LEADING CONTEMPORARY POETS

AN INTERNATIONAL ANTHOLOGY

LEADING CONTEMPORARY POETS

AN INTERNATIONAL ANTHOLOGY

Edited by

DASHA ČULIĆ NISULA

ASSOCIATE EDITORS:

Sunny Jung, Asia
Ellen Hinsey, Western Europe
Douglas Jones, Canada
Daniel Kunene, Africa
Eric Sellin, Francophone Africa

Printed in the United States of America

First Edition

ISBN: 0-9657851-0-6

POETRY INTERNATIONAL
Department of Foreign Languages and Literatures
Western Michigan University
Kalamazoo, Michigan 49008-5091

In memory

of

Elizabeth Bartlett

I am the teacher of athletes,

He that by me spreads a wider

breast than my own proves the

width of my own,

He most honors my style

who learns under it

to destroy the teacher.

Walt Whitman
Leaves of Grass

TABLE OF CONTENTS

INTRODUCTION

CONGO:

CROATIA:

9

RUSSIA

SLOVENIA

UKRAINE

UNITED STATES

14

INTRODUCTION

This anthology is the fourth in the series of international anthologies published every four years coinciding with the Olympic Games. The idea of honoring mental prowess as we do physical was initiated by Elizabeth Bartlett, a recognized poet in her own right, who edited the first three volumes of this series in 1984, 1988 and 1992. Midway in the process of preparing the fourth collection, however, Elizabeth Bartlett suddenly became ill and died in 1994. Just as unexpectedly I found myself to be the next editor for this 1996 volume. I had the privilege to act as an Associate Editor for the Central Europe portion of the 1992 volume in the series, and I am now pleased to have been asked to continue the project, one that Ms. Bartlett held so close to her heart.

After considering several working titles for this collection, the final decision was to accept *Leading Contemporary Poets: An International Anthology*. This volume commemorates the 100th anniversary of the Games in modern times. I am delighted to point out that it brings together over one hundred poems from over twenty different countries, translated from over fifteen different languages. Poets included in this volume range from countries as close as Canada and Mexico and as distant as Bosnia and Zimbabwe. No matter where they are from, the poets in this anthology have come together to honor and bid farewell to Elizabeth Bartlett. This volume then, first and foremost, is a memorial to a poet and a colleague whose project has given voice to those who would otherwise remain unheard by the ever increasing English speaking audience.

Just as athletes from the newly independent countries marched out in the opening ceremony at the Olympic Games in 1996, so this volume too has a good representation of poets from such newly independent countries as Croatia, Latvia and Ukraine. In addition, one may note that in this volume there are included up to eight poems by a single poet. Where earlier anthologies in this series emphasized breadth of representation across a large number of countries, the present anthology seeks to give the reader a look of some depth into the work of individual poets.

Because the Olympic Games of 1996 took place in the States, Elizabeth Bartlett thought that the United States should have strong representation in this volume. The anthology contains the work of eleven American poets, some previously unpublished. As for the foreign poets, their work appears here for the first time in English translation. Two poets died while this collection was in progress. One is an American poet, James Merrill, who died on February 6, 1995; the other is a Romanian poet, Marin Sorescu, who died on December 8, 1996. May this collection serve as a memorial to them as well.

Begun in the spring of 1995, this project now nears completion. I would like to take this opportunity to thank all the poets and translators who have given their support to this project by generously submitting their work and all individuals whose financial contributions have made the publication of this volume possible. Secondly, I am grateful for the help I received from the members of the American Literary Translators Association and the Associate Editors for this edition: Sunny B. Jung of the University of California-San Diego; Ellen Hinsey, recognized by the 1996 Yale Series of Younger Poets; Douglas Jones of Canada; Daniel Kunene of the University of Wisconsin; and Eric Selene of Tulane University. Thirdly, I am indebted to our department secretary, Elaine Gaudio, for her patience and competence and who, after multiple renditions of Russian, Ukrainian and Romanian poems, is still at her job. I also wish to thank Marko Marjanović and Eric Nisula for their help in reading either originals and/or the English translations. The Department of Foreign Languages and Literatures at Western Michigan University also deserves recognition for providing support to bring this project to completion. Last, but not least, I wish to thank Steven Bartlett who first asked me to work on this project, who guided me along the way, and who gave me a free hand at what and how much could be included. I am also happy he has been able to provide heretofore unpublished poems by Elizabeth Bartlett and the afterword for this anthology.

D. C. N.

DIVIDED LAND

Vahakn Davtian

My divided land, my undivided heart
I am doubled over by my debts to you.
Like true conscience I ache with pity
festering like an unhealing wound.

What shall I say, I who was born too late?
I should have shed blood for you
like the blood drained fedayi
in the icy mountains of Erzeroum.

Sleeping, no, dozing only,
as heartaches and sorrows doze
like the volcano keeping alive
its beating heart a flaming rose.

I should have been mingled with your soil
blended with the terrible cries
blistered into one flame in the eternal fire
when your resurrected ruins rise.

But you gave birth to me too late
to fight. I should have bled
not remained a passive ache
inside a festering unhealed wound.

tr. Diana Der-Hovanessian

Vahakn Davtian
Armenia

ENOUGH TO MAKE HIM HOWL

Vahakn Davtian

Black beams, black walls,
black dusk, black dawn,
In the bleak darkness,
the sound of stifled sobs.

— Jesus, barefoot Jesus,
this place is full of thorns.
You come in vain to this land.
Beware of these sharp stones.

Black clouds in our hearts;
black snow, black hail.
How will we shelter a god
who is bloodied like us?

Black posts, black walls,
black dawn, black dusk.
And in the bleak darkness
the sound of stifled sobs.

— Jesus, barefoot Jesus,
your path is strewn with thorns.
Your long robe trails blood
and yet you remain calm.

If you insist on coming,
then come to our blessed home.
This time the suffering you will see
is enough to make you moan.

tr. Diana Der-Hovanessian

Gevorg Emin
Armenia

WINTER STEW

Gevorg Emin

To prepare a bozbash
all you need is lamb
meat and two onions
thinly sliced.
All you need is satin
cabbage coarsely chopped,
salt, cumin, pepper and
oh, I almost forgot
the most soul stirring
spice, the delicious secret
ingredient found only
in one single strand
of gray hair fallen
from your mother's head.

tr. Diana Der-Hovanessian

WINTER

by Bedros Horasanjian

To be a fish and not need water,
to be a bird and not sail on air,
to be a forest and give up green,
to be a mountain and hate the stones,
to be springtime and change your name,
to be a child not needing play,
to be Lord Byron forgetting Greece,
to be human and not need man,
that is when true winter comes.

tr. Diana Der-Hovanessian

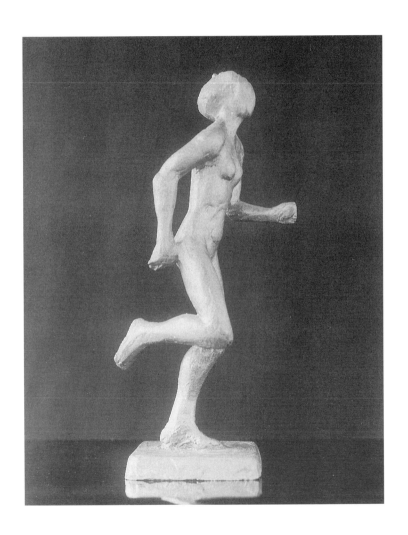

{LE POÈTE}

Roger Aralamon Hazoume

Le/Poète/en faisant/exploser/les mots/et/le Verbe/
Découvre/le monde/dans/ses limbes/incantatoires/
Et/voici/que/la vie rafale/la vie vampire/la vie/
En/déroulant/ses longues feuilles/repliées/comme/
des/souffrances/avortées/
Apprivoise/le poète/dans/les sillons/du langage/fantôme/
Et/la nuit/s'étend/sur/la mer/houleuse/pleine/
de sons/et/de paroles/hurlements/cyclones/
Et/dans/son lit/le poète/investi/du pouvoir/
symbolique/des griots/mandingues/traverse/
les fleuves/les champs/les forêts/et/les villages/
à/la recherche/de la source/primordiale/

{THE POET}

by Roger Aralamon Hazoume

The/Poet/by causing/words/and/the Word/to explode/
Discovers/the world/in his/incantatory/limbo/
And/behold/how/the tempestuous life/the soul devouring life/life/
By unfurling/her long/wilted/leaves/like/many/miscarried/sufferings/
Tames/the poet/in/the furrows/of an elusive/language/
And/the night/spreads itself/across/the turbulent/sea/of many/
sounds/and voices/screams/cyclonic winds/
And/in/his bed/the poet/endowed/with/the symbolic/
power/of the Malinke/griots/crosses over/
the rivers/the plains/the forests/and/the villages/
towards/the discovery/of the primordial/origin/

tr. Stephanie Yang

KADA SE SMIJU OBIČNE ŽENE ATENSKE

Bisera Alikadić

Kao da su zaboravile sve obaveze, sva zla.
Neobuzdano se smiju sebi, muškaricima,
Djeci, natopljenim pelenicama,
Suncu, krilatici drage im pokojnice.
Njihov smijeh je bujica, nalet slobode.
Blistavi vrt pod srcem vasione.
Ovoj iskonskoj radosti ravno nije
Ni krdo mladih konja kad izvija grive.
To je blagdan,
Sveopšti potop razdraganosti.
Poezija čula u bezbrižnoj razigranosti.
Grudi im se razlivaju na sve strane.
Oči pretvaraju u linije ravne.
Jata zubi bljesnu, pa nestanu ko ptice.
Da pod zemlju polugu stave
Zavaljale bi je kao tešku kuglu.
O, sreće, kada se smiju,
Kao da more navire,
Kao da se nebeski vidici šire.
Šta li nam to život
Kroz njihov zvonki smijeh poručuje?

WHEN ORDINARY ATHENIAN WOMEN LAUGH

by Bisera Alikadić

As if they've forgotten all responsibilities, all evil.
Unrestrainedly they laugh at themselves, men,
Children, soaked diapers,
The sun, quotes of their dearly departed.
Their laughter is a torrent, a gust of freedom,
A radiant garden under the heart of the universe.
This primeval happiness is not even similar to
A herd of young horses as they shake their manes.
That's a holiday,
A universal deluge of joy,
Poetry of sense in careless excitement.
Their breasts pour over on all sides,
Their eyes turn into straight lines,
A flock of teeth flash, then disappear like birds.
If they were to put a lever under ground
They would roll it like a heavy ball.
Oh, happiness, when they laugh,
As if the sea flows out,
As if celestial landscapes widen.
What is life telling us
Through their ringing laughter?

tr. Dasha Čulić Nisula

Margaret Atwood
Canada

HEART

Margaret Atwood

Some people sell their blood. You sell your heart.
It was either that or the soul.
The hard part is getting the darn thing out.
A kind of twisting motion, like shucking an oyster,
your whole spine a wrist,
and then, hup! It's in your mouth.
You turn yourself partially inside out
Like a sea anemone coughing a pebble;
There's a broken plop, the racket
of fish guts into a pail,
and there it is, a huge glistening deep-red clot
of the still-alive past, whole on the plate.

It gets passed around. It's slippery. It gets dropped
but also tasted. Too salty, says one. Too sweet.
Too sour, says another, making a face.
Each one is an instant gourmet,
and you stand listening to all this
in the corner, like a newly-hired waiter,
your diffident, skillful hand on the wound hidden
deep in your shirt and chest,
shyly, heartless.

LE PRÉSENT PEUT DURER

Normand de Bellefeuille

Le présent peut durer
puisqu'il y a les mots du présent
et même les pires mots
du présent comme
**le ciel est mortel qui se peigne de
quelques branches**
ou alors
**le ciel n'est que le vent vu
par-dessous**
doivent nous en convaincre:
le présent peut durer
car il ne s'agit peut-être tout compte fait
que de désobéir aux morts
que de mille boîtes retournées
dans notre corps
dans la partie chantée de notre corps
cet oiseau ordinaire

le présent peut durer
mais il ne nous faut en attendre
rien d'autre que le tonnerre
rien d'autre que les pires mots du présent
car c'est sur ses bords
que la parole fait mal
alors que ceux qui hésitent
ferment leurs fenêtres

THE PRESENT CAN LAST

by Normand de Bellefeuille

The present can last
since there are the words of the present
and even the worst words
of the present, like
**the heavens are mortal grooming themselves
with a few branches**
or else
**the heavens are only the wind
seen from below**
ought to convince us:
the present can last
for perhaps, all things considered
it's only a question of disobeying the dead
of a thousand boxes in our body
turned over
in the sung parts of our body
this ordinary bird

the present can last
though we must expect
nothing less than its thunder
nothing less than the worst words of the present
for it's on its edges
speech hurts
while those who hesitate
close their windows

tr. D. G. Jones

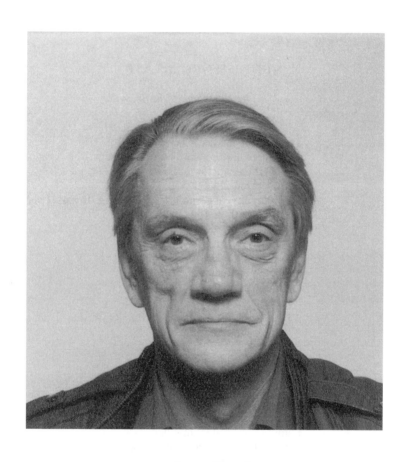

George Bowering
Canada

NORWEGIAN LINES

George Bowering

Lars showed me
the grand boulevard
downtown Oslo.

They were making
artificial ice
for skating on.

How wonderful
imagination
upside down.

Lars told me
turn Norway over
it reaches Rome.

Norse get lost
finding hotels
or far continents.

Those lucky leaves
home in Oslo
crunch underfoot.

Lars found me
a downstairs bar
with dark brown beer.

Eating peanuts
dark November
how delightful.

It's a saga
told in minutes
Sonja Henie.

ÉLOGE DE L'INCONNU

François Charron

si la parole nous dissimule
si la parole n'est plus qu'une habitude parmi tant d'autres
si la parole ne signifie plus qu'une apparence inécoutée

alors à nouveau se présentera, étrangère à cette parole,
la faiblesse inattendue du poème

alors à nouveau ressurgira ce point vibrant et disponible
qui se divise un million de fois pour rester lui-même
— cette seule minute libre désormais
de toute raréfaction consacrée de l'être

mieux que personne, un clair matin de mai salue ici,
ô encre de nudité, la chère lueur d'un silence <u>matériel</u>

IN PRAISE OF THE UNKNOWN

by François Charron

if speech is our dissembling
if speech is but a habit among so many others
if speech is but an index of something unheard

then, afresh, and stranger to this speech, the unexpected
weakness of the poem will stand out

then, afresh, this vibrant and readily available point
that divides a million times over and remains itself
will resurface — this single minute free now
from all consecrated rarefaction of being

better than anyone, here, a bright May morning greets
o ink of nakedness, the cherished lustre of a material silence

tr. D. G. Jones

François Charron
Canada

Madeleine Gagnon
Canada

REMINISCENCES[*]

Madeleine Gagnon

"Le poète fit à l'homme son premier cadeau:
il dessina un rocher tombant
du haut d'une falaise. Celui-ci, en se brisant
sur le sol, libéra dix mille PIERRES."

(Pierre Aroneanu, *Le Maître des Signes*)

J'entends le chant de la terre, on me croirait assise sur sa plus haute falaise,
    j'entends
La galerie est de travertin, marbré de rose, d'ocre et d'opale, j'entends
    jusque dans ma main
La main caresse cette poudre calcaire, ruiselle à mon tympan le bruit de la
    matière
Plus bas, très loin, la mer, ce pourrait être l'Atlantique mais c'est l'Égée
    d'enfance imaginée
J'entends le chant de la terre, tous les espaces m'habitent, l'oreille n'a pas de
    frontières
Au nord du 49e parallèle, sur la plus haute falaise de grès sédimenté,
    j'entends le chant de la terre
Mes doigts suivent le filet rouge, mes doigts cherchent la mémoire des âges
    sous le quartz érodé
Sur le grain veineux, je palpe une brèche sonore, j'entends le chant de la terre
Par-delà tout désastre entrevu, au bord du gouffre nucléaire
Rivant le corps entier au moindre souffle chu des pulsations d'astres
    J'entends le chant de la terre
A mes pieds dans ce Nord tout juste frigorifié que le printemps encore
    rechauffe
Je vois, ramassé foetal en plein conglomérat, tassé au sein du galet de silex
L'image d'une sphère vivante, douée d'yeux et de bouche avec, enfouie
    comme en un songe
Une oreille qui vibre et qui écoute, je sais, je prends la roche au creux de ma
    main
J'entends le chant de la terre

---

[*] En écoutant "La Chant de la Terre" de Gustav Mahler

REMINISCENCES*

by Madeleine Gagnon

> "The poet gave man his first gift: he
> sketched a rock falling from
> the height of a cliff: shattering
> on the ground below, it
> liberated ten thousand STONES."
>
> (Pierre Aroneanu, *Le Maître des Signes*)

I hear the song of the earth, as if I were sitting on its highest cliff,
    I hear
The gallery is travertine, marbled with rose, ochre and opal, I hear even
    through my hand
My hand strokes this powdery limestone, through my ear drum streams the
    sound of matter
Lower down, far off, the sea, it could be the Atlantic but it's the imagined
    Aegean of childhood
I hear the song of the earth, all regions find habitation within me, the ear
    knows no borders
North of the 49th parallel, on the highest cliff of sedimentary rock, I hear
    the song of the earth
My fingers follow the red filiation, my fingers seek the memory of eons
    under the eroded quartz
On the arterial grain, I tap a sonorous fault, I hear the song of the earth
Beyond all foreseen disasters, on the brink of the nuclear abyss
Binding the whole body with the least breath fallen from the pulsing stars
    I hear the song of the earth
At my feet, in this North, frostbound but lately, spring working to warm
    it, I see
Gathered and foetal in the midst of conglomerate rock,
    lodged in the flinty heart of the shingle
The image of a living sphere, endowed with eyes and with a mouth and,
    burrowed as in a dream
With an ear, vibrant and listening, I know, I take the rock in the hollow
    of my hand
  I hear the song of the earth

tr. D.G. Jones

---

*While listening to Mahler's "The Song of the Earth"

Patrick Lane
Canada

COUGAR

Patrick Lane

The cougar before she falls from her high limb
holds for one moment the ponderosa pine, her back
arched, her tail so still the forest stops.
There are silences to learn,
each one an invocation: the one that follows
a father's rage at a child, a woman's rage at man,
a child's tears you watch as if the sound
was a language you must learn. But a cougar's falling?
Nothing is so quiet. Even the wind stops to listen.
Beetles, busy at death, lift up their jointed legs,
whiskey-jacks slide quietly away, and ravens appear
as if they had been made out of the air.
It is to watch a thing whose only gift is death
give to herself, feeling the explosion in her heart
a thing she has made and not the men below
and not the dogs as they watch her falling
through the limbs and then erupting into sound,
their hard mouths biting what is already dead.
It is the boy on a horse so old it will not run,
a boy who watches, not understanding the men
who, when she falls, shoot their rifles at the sun,
as if with such exultance
they could bring a darkness into the world.

Daphne Marlatt
Canada

{PHOTO}

Daphne Marlatt

photo / graphing you a

      water dance it glimmers brilliant
track incessant form diaphanous wing this light swarm being
draws, soft curve of cheek, arm, hair

            illumined white

the solid wood of roof support encased erased in wave iota glint

not literal love shimmers its biosphere some distant blue familiar
lines do recognize cheek, lash, light

          hold us within it, this
is home i want you deep in the whole of, arms outstretched like fins
shaped pure alabaster light or quartz there in your eye, hair flown
off the rail and into polar dazzle constellated in the deep of you
small lucid bear aplay on a floe just off (the porch) beyond
(Vesuvius) and through the corner of your eyes'

           ferocious light

P. K. Page
Canada

FUNERAL MASS

P. K. Page

In his blackest suit
the father carries the coffin

It is light as a box of kleenex
He carries it in one hand

It is white and gold
A jewel box

Their baby is in it

In the unconscionable weather
the father sweats and weeps

The mother leans
on the arms of two women friends

By the sacred light of the church
they are pale as gristle

The priests talk Latin
change their elaborate clothes

their mitres, copes
their stoles embroidered by nuns

Impervious to grief
their sole intention

is the intricate ritual
of returning a soul to God

this sinless homunculus
this tiny seed

L'ÂGE DES MARÉES

Jean-Baptiste Tati-Loutard

Je cherche l'âge des marées
Parmi les terrains vagues
D'où la mer s'est retirée
Oubliant les mouvements des vagues
       dans le sable
Et la blancheur d'écume aux commissures
       des coquillages;
Jusqu'aux derniers éclats des lames
Le sel plus lourd de la terre
Donne une herbe grasse
Des retombées d'embrun
Où ne germe point de sueur paysanne.
La mer engloutit jadis quelques rivages;
Légère est la charge des souvenirs
       d'une vie d'homme
Sans le poids du Livre des Morts
Où manque l'âge des marées.

THE AGE OF TIDES

by Jean-Baptiste Tati-Loutard

I try to read the age of tides
Among the waste lands
Whence the sea has ebbed
Forgetting the waves' motion in the sand
And the seaspray's whiteness by the seashell's cleft;
Until the very last scintillation on the waves
The heavier salt of the earth
Yields a grass thickened
By the spindrift's fallout
Where no farmer's sweat takes seed.
In olden times the sea devoured shores;
Light is the burden of one man's memories
Without the weight of the Book of the Dead
Which fails to mention the age of tides.

tr. Eric Sellin

FEUX ET RUINES

Jean-Baptiste Tati-Loutard

D'un soleil à l'autre je descends les marches
vers les ruines;
J'aborde aux premières blancheurs de l'âge,
Barque tirée au sec
Sur un fond d'écume non repris par la mer.
Les arbres le pépiement des feuillages
Me donnent le goût d'un autre destin:
Une vie d'oiseau non comestible perdu
Au séjour des folles essences.
J'ai vécu en des lieux où la femme seule
Porte le sac-au-dos du soleil des champs,
Perd le souffle à la cueillette des fruits.
Nous avons construit nos villages en des bois
Où fermentaient des Esprits.
Où sont les jours d'éclipse, les nuits de deuil
Pour cause de blasphèmes?
Il se fait un doux sommeil sous l'arbre à midi
Paisible dans la paix du jour.
Et pourquoi des cieux bouleversés,
Des nuages de feu
Qui montent des Saïgon et des Beyrouth?
Sommes-nous encore l'herbe des champs
Que l'on brûle?

FIRES AND RUINS

by Jean-Baptiste Tati-Loutard

From one sun to the next I descend the steps toward the ruins;
I approach the first pale glimmer of the age,
A boat pulled up on the beach
On a base of foam not reclaimed by the sea.
The trees the chirping of the foliage
Provide me with the taste of a different destiny:
The life of an inedible bird lost
In the residence of wild essences.
I have lived in places where only women
Bear the backpack of sunlit fields,
Grow breathless gathering fruit.
We built our villages in forests
Where the Spirits teemed.
Where are the days of eclipse, the nights of grieving
Over blasphemies?
One can know sweet slumber under the tree at noon
Peaceful in the calm of day.
And why these churning skies,
These fiery clouds
Rising from the Saigons and Beiruts?
Are we once again but field grass
Only good for burning?

tr. Eric Sellin

LA VIE

Jean-Baptiste Tati-Loutard

Nous sommes sur terre à la fenêtre
D'un train de nuit:
L'herbe perçoit le mouvement et non le visage.

LIFE

by Jean-Baptiste Tati-Loutard

Here on earth we are by the window
Of a night train:
The grass detects the movement but not the face.

tr. Eric Sellin

FOUDRE

Jean-Baptiste Tati-Loutard

Dans le salon le temps jouait
Ferme avec sa boîte à musique
Quand la poudrière s'embrasa
Et la bibliothèque où manuscrits et défets
Devinrent les premiers oiseaux de feu.

LIGHTNING

by Jean-Baptiste Tati-Loutard

In the living room the weather played
Loudly on its music box
When the powder-magazine began to blaze
As did the library in which manuscripts
and balled-up cast-off pages
Became the first birds of flame.

tr. Eric Sellin

SÉDUCTION VÉGÉTALE

Jean-Baptiste Tati-Loutard

Dans mon adolescence quelque peu lointaine
J'étais jaloux d'un arbre qui plaisait
Aux femmes dans les après-midi torrides
Le vent leur faisait un éventail
De ses branches pleines de fraîcheur
Et le soleil changeait le feuillage
En un cabinet de tatouage.

SÉDUCTION VÉGÉTALE

by Jean-Baptiste Tati-Loutard

In my somewhat distant youth
I envied a tree that women were drawn to
In the torrid afternoons
The wind offered them a fan
In the cool-filled branches
And the sun turned the foliage
Into an outdoor tattoo parlour.

tr. Eric Sellin

DISANJE

Neda Miranda Blažević

Počela sam disati
kao netko tko se
veseli prvim koracima.
Tvoji besprijekorni
zahtjevi, srce,
sada me ne mogu stići.
Moj je dah lukaviji
dublji, premda ga noću
ponekad još gubim
prestrašena bezobličnim
zadatkom koji trebam
ispuniti.
Prije nekoliko dana,
sjedim na obali Jezera
i ti kažeš: plivaj
s ovom košarom na glavi.
U hladnoj vodi
košara s ručkom i pićem
pritišće mi tjeme
i ja tonem gušeći se.
Ali vježbam
vježbam disanje
duboko i ritmično.
Gotovo da uspijevam.

BREATHING

by Neda Miranda Blažević

I began to breathe
as one elated
with the first steps.
Your irreproachable
demands, dear,
cannot reach me now.
My breath is craftier
deeper, though at night
I still sometimes lose it,
frightened by the formless
assignment which I must
fulfill.
A few days ago,
I sit at the shore of a Lake
and you say: swim
with this basket on your head.
In cold water
the basket with lunch and drink
presses on the top of my head
and I sink suffocating.
But I practice
I practice breathing
deeply and rhythmically.
I am almost successful.

tr. Dasha Čulić Nisula

HAPPY NEW YORK 1985

Neda Miranda Blažević

Sir i krekeri
umak "Bella Donna"
odresci a la Stroganoff
riža s gljivama
miješana salata
crveno vino "Yvon Man"
salata od voća
Sacher torta
šampanjac.
Jestivi krajolik polegnut
na novogodišnja koljena
istom težinom
bojom o točnošću kojima je
Maljevič gurnuo perspektivu
na rub Novog Stoljeća.
Između svijeća
gori razlika u vremenu
u šarenom okusu
koji nas jede
koji jedemo
u pravilnim razmacima.
Ti ne jedeš.
Gledaš kroz prozor
kristal Manhattana
što nas zasipa hladno
hladno sa svih strana.

HAPPY NEW YORK 1985

by Neda Miranda Blažević

Cheese and crackers
"Bella Donna" dip
cuts a la Stroganoff
rice with mushrooms
mixed salad
red wine "Yvon Man"
fruit salad
Sacher torte
champagne.
An edible scenery laid out
at New Year's knees
in same weight
color of exactness with which
Malevich pushed the perspective
to the edge of the New Century.
Between the candles
burns the difference in time
in multicolored taste
which eats us
who eat
in exact intervals.
You're not eating.
You're looking through the window
at the crystal Manhattan
that fills us coldly
coldly from all sides.

tr. Dasha Čulić Nisula

Neda Miranda Blažević
Croatia

Nada Iveljić
Croatia

SADA SMO SIGURNI

Nada Iveljić

Pažljivo zatvaram vrata svoga stana
Namičem prst debeo lanac
Na lancu golem lokot
Kao što je red
Sigurna od kradljivaca
ubojica i lopova
pašljivo zatvaram vrata svoga stana

A onaj koji je oduvijek krao
taj tip neprepoznatljiv
taj lopov na sve spreman
i ubojica s licem ljupke zore
već leži crn u mojoj bijeloj postelji
i kaže: Baš dobro
Sada smo sigurni
Nitko nam više neće smetati

NOW WE ARE SAFE

by Nada Iveljić

Carefully I close the door of my home
I put on a finger-thick chain
On the chain a huge lock
As must be done
To be safe from thieves
murderers and rogues
carefully I close the door of my home

But the one who has always stolen
that undetectable type
that rogue ready for anything
and a murderer with a face of sweet dawn
already lies wicked in my white bed
and says: Really good
Now we are safe
No one will bother us anymore

tr. Dasha Čulić Nisula

DOBA MILOSTI

Nada Iveljić

Danas mogu mirno pružiti ruke preda se
Ne zabrinjava me daleka tutnjava. Ništa nemam
Što bih mogla izgubiti i moje srce može lako
Savladati dugu noć punu užasa
Znam da se u njoj psi otimaju s lanaca
A samotnici grizu jastuke
Moj pogled je u ravnini mjeseca, dok su
Iza njega ostala poplavljena proljeća mladosti
I dno košare, prošupljeno
Od teških jabuka
Ključem sjećanja otvaram vrata prošlosti
Izlijeću uspomene osramoćene i čašćene
Vapaji i uzdisaji, sreća na koljenima
I sreća osovljena

Ali odjednom se sve mijenja. Nastupilo je
Doba milosti. Nema boli ni trzanja
Ruže u njedrima mirišu blago i privrženo
Vodopadi ne huče. Samo trpka radost
Življenja teče polako
Srebrna i gusta kao olovna rijeka
Na jednom dlanu držim srce
Na drugom svijet. U ravnoteži su
I ljubim ih takve kakvi jesu, ma i razoreni

THE AGE OF MERCY

by Nada Iveljić

Today I can peacefully extend my arms
I am not concerned about the distant thunder. I have nothing
To lose and my heart can easily
Bear the long night full of terror
In which I know the dogs pull at the chains
And the lonely bite pillows
My glance is at the level of the moon, while behind
It remain sunken springs of youth
And the bottom of a basket, broken
By heavy apples
I open the door of the past with a key of remembrance
Memories pour out disgraced and revered
Screams and sighs, happiness on its knees
And happiness raised upright

But suddenly all changes. The age of mercy
Arrived. There is no pain or spasm
Roses in the bosom smell softly and faithfully
The waterfalls do not roar. Only the bitter joy
Of existence flows slowly
Silver and thick like a leaden river
On one palm I hold my heart
On the other the world. They balance
And I love them as they are, even though destroyed.

tr. Dasha Čulić Nisula

TITIVILLUS

Nada Iveljić

Iz mraka dalekih stoljeća iznesoše pismenost
strpljivi prepisivači
Uz žmirkavu svjetlost lojanica
brojni Gligoriji i Bartoli pogrbljeni
nad stranicama lekcionara, oficija, molitvenika
vješti kaligrafi i minijaturisti
ostaviše iza sebe prve knjige
dokaz stanja ondašnjeg duha i jezika
narodnoga, pismenosti glagoljske i
latiničke, iskre umjetnosti

A Titivillus, vražićak napasni, njihov Tintilinić
strašio ih kugom, ratom i vječnim mrakom
navodeći ih da zapišu na margini
riječi nimalo sakralne, kao: žedan sam
gladan, dosta mi je, hoću spavati
pa benediktince i ine redovnike izrugujući
(fratri, fračetiri, fradevet, fra-u-krevet)
svjetovnu ljepotu Krbave veličajući
te ostalih naših krajeva vinorodnih
šaptao im o Prometeju Gutenbergu
o tisku koji će njihov rad obezvrijediti

Doći će vrijeme, peckao je
ispoštene i malovide
kad će ljudi na tone ispisana papira
danomice bacati u otpad
Djelo vaše — sekundarna sirovina, govoraše
A oni njemu: Apage, Sotonin potomče
Opat nas mori glađu zbog svake greške

TITIVILLUS

by Nada Iveljić

Out of dark distant centuries literacy was brought
forward by patient copiers
By the blinking light of tallow-candles
numerous Grigorys and Bartols hunched
over the pages of lectionary, services, prayer books
dexterous calligraphers and miniaturists
left behind them the first books
evidence of the time's spirit and language
of the people, literacy in Glagolitic and
Latin, sparks of art

But Titivillus, a tempting little devil, their Titivilly
frightened them all with war and eternal darkness
telling them to write down in the margins
words hardly sacred, as: I am thirsty
hungry, I had enough, I want to sleep
and ridiculing Benedictines and other monks
(friar, briar, get thee to a choir)
extolling worldly beauty of Krbava
and the rest of our wine-growing regions
he whispered to them about Prometheus Gutenberg
about a text which will invalidate their work

Time will come, he teased
ascetics and myopes
when the people will throw daily to waste
tons of written paper
Your work is secondary raw material, he said
And they to him: Get thee hence Satan's descendant
Abbot tortures us with hunger for each mistake

I slova se nizahu skladno kao biseri u ogrlice
namirući nam u baštinu svevremensku istinu

Tako naše telo mine
Tako naša slava gine

And the letters fall in a row like pearls on a necklace
providing us an inheritance of eternal truth

Thus our body vanishes
Thus our glory perishes

tr. Dasha Čulić Nisula

SAT ENGLESKE LEKTIRE

Božica Jelušić

Hodajući kroz jednu šumu by OSCAR WILDE
upoznali smo razne životinje i bilje
brali smo gljive čudnih oblika, divnih boja
od kojih je, međutim, većina bila otrovna
po čemu smo uočili vjerodostojnost tvrdnje
da je Književnost samo jedan odraz života
a izvukli smo (usput) još neke mudre pouke
sasvim neupotrebljive

Neki su zbilja bili užasno nepristojni
drugarica je stalno vikala Dosta, dosta
vratite se vi napredni, LAWRENCE ove godine
još nije u programu

No usprkos tim moralno labilnim elementima
bio je to još jedan besmrtan sat lektire
a najveću su zbrku stvorile štreberice
koje su ispod strašno divljeg kestena našle
staroga TRESIKRUŠKU (zvanog SHAKES-PEAR-e)
kako hrče, bez imalo osjećaja za ritam

džepova punih lišća i toalet—papira
na kojima su pisali neki još neobjavljeni
ali po svemu sudeći
izvanredni soneti.

A CLASS IN ENGLISH LITERATURE

by Božica Jelušić

Walking through a forest by OSCAR WILDE
we learned about different animals and plants
we picked strangely shaped mushrooms, in beautiful color
most of which were, however, poisonous
from which we deduced the authenticity of the claim
that Literature is only one reflection of life.
We extricated, along the way, some other wise lessons
completely useless

Some were really terribly rude
the professor continuously shouted Enough, enough
you advanced return, this year LAWRENCE is
not on the program yet

But in spite of these morally unstable elements
that was still another immortal lit class
but the biggest confusion created the crammers
who under a huge horse chestnut found
the old PEARSHAKER (called SHAKES-PEAR-e)
snoring, without any regard for rhythm

pockets full of leaves and toilet paper
on which were written some still unpublished
but judging by everything
extraordinary sonnets.

tr. Dasha Čulić Nisula

MASTER WILLIAM

Božica Jelušić

Master William, divlja kruška
kompilator, falokrat
prevrtljiva vjera muška
suknjolovac — topli brat

što je pis'o kvareć' rime
o vremenu svom bez maske
na sceni je jedne zime
rek'o mjereć' trule daske:

"Biti sada, il' ne bit?"
Pisat', gorjet' knjige štit
dok te kuša Slava — zmija?

Il' pod perinu se skrit'
biti blažen, svega sit
i uzdisat' (a kaj drugo?)

POST COITUM TRISTITIA?

MASTER WILLIAM

by Božica Jelušić

Master William, wild pear
compiler, phallocrat,
changeable man's faith,
skirtchaser — queer

who wrote corrupt rhyme
about his time without a mask
on the stage one winter he
said looking at the rotten boards:

"To be now, or not to be?"
Write, burn book covers
while Fame tempts you — the snake?

Or hide under the covers,
be blissful, full of everything
and sigh (and what else?)

POST COITUM TRISTITIA?

tr. Dasha Čulić Nisula

7.

Anka Žagar

gdje sam bila, a gdje, a zašto
ne pitaš tramvaje gdje su bili
GUAR
stajala sam
između njih dvojice
da ne zapljusnu, plavi
jedan drugomu
u lice

toliko me je naime bilo
tamo da, ovdje ne

GUAR, trčala sam po sebi
mi nemamo vremena, a za vas
još ne znam

kako jesen dolazi, kako će
sigurno doći samo ne znam
kojim će tramvajem, kojim
riječima ako te
prestanem voljeti

GUAR, nazvat ćeš ovu eteričnu sliku
urezati kao jutarnje tračnice, kao
beskrajni okvir za
umjetnost praznine

7.

by Anka Žagar

where was I, but where, and why
you don't ask the trams where they were
GUAR
I stood
between the two of them
so they don't splash
at each other's
face

that's how much there was of me
there yes, here no

GUAR, I was running over myself
we don't have time, and for you
I still don't know

how autumn approaches, how it will
surely come, but I don't know
by what tram, in what
words if I
stop loving you

GUAR, you'll call this ethereal picture
engrave it like the morning rails, like
the endless frame for
the art of emptiness

tr. Dasha Čulić Nisula

15.

Anka Žagar

slušala sam žito
slušala sam žito

da se nahrani životinja
da se nahrani životinja

ponavljalo je žuto
ponavljalo je žito
pa ponavljam i ja

jer ne razumijem
pjesmu
kad je zrela

ali ne, ni ja
ne idem nikamo
zemlja sama
ide
pod mojim nogama

15.

by Anka Žagar

I listened to the corn
I listened to the corn

to feed the animal
to feed the animal

it repeated yellow
it repeated corn
and so I repeat too

because I don't understand
the song
when it's ripe

but no, neither do I
go anywhere
the earth alone
goes
under my feet

tr. Dasha Čulić Nisula

Tyyne Saastamoinen
Finland

Tyyne Saastamoinen

Elämän syvät virrat, luulin että tyrehdytte iän mukana;
pelkäsin käyväni kuivaksi kuin erämaa tai upottavaksi kuin
suo, mutta tässä minä olen ajatusteni kanssa tuoreena ja
virkeänä ja kuka laskisi ikääni, ei, annan sen olla, ei se ole
poikkipäin tielläni vaan vastassa kuin suuri viuhka, tehty
suurista sulista paratiisin portilla juuri minua varten. Tai
kuin purppuraviitta se on harteillani, jokaisesta päivästä
minä iloitsen ja päivät kiertyvät viikoiksi ja kuukausiksi ja
sitten ovat vuodet, suuret rypäleet joista olen puristanut
mehun. Viiniä se on minun pikarissani, vuosikertani viiniä,
helmeilevää, hyvää. Ja jokaisessa pullossa korkki ja tynny-
rissä tappi taitavaa työtä taitavasti irrotettavaksi. Pidot
minä pidän ikäni saartamana ja ylistän isääni suuren talon
miestä, itseäni suuremman, ja äitiäni kalastajan tytärtä,
lapsuuteni emäntää, kielen ilosta minä iloitsen ja kiitän
vaikka ilta on myöhä, väki yhä pellolla ja lyhteet painavat.

by Tyyne Saastamoinen

Deep currents of life, I thought that you would exhaust with age;
I was afraid of becoming dry like a desert or soft like a marsh,
but here I am with my thoughts—fresh and alert, and who would
think to count my years, no, I let them go—age doesn't block my
way but welcomes like a great fan, just for me, made from immense
feathers, waiting at the door of paradise. Or like a crimson cloak on
my shoulders—I praise each day, and the days roll into weeks and
months, and then there are the years—large clusters of grapes from
which I press the juice. Wine is in my glass, the wine of my year—
sparkling, good. And in each bottle there is a cork, and in each barrel
a well-tailored stopper that releases with a simple twist. I make
a banquet surrounded by my age, and I praise my father, the man
of the big house, bigger than me, and my mother, the daughter
of a fisherman, the mistress of my childhood; I rejoice in the joy
of language, and I give thanks: even if it is late, there are still
workers in the field, and the sheaves are heavy.

tr. Ellen Hinsey &
Heini Vartia-Delafont

Tyyne Saastamoinen

Minä elän näitä hiljaisia sanojani niin kuin elän hiljaisia
päiviäni, hitaasti nousen ylämäkeä tai liu'un rinnettä,
joskus olen paikallani kuin paalu tai kivi, pantu merkiksi
kulkijalle, nämä runoni minä syön ja juon ja myön ja nämä
ovat omiani niin kuin sormieni ja varpaitteni kynnet tai
putoavat päästäni niin kuin hiukset kammatessa, harmaita
ne alkavat jo olla mutta voin minä sitoa myös punaisen
nauhan hiuksiini itseni iloksi ja kun kuolen toivon olevani
kuin Hölderlin puusepän sitoma seppele päässä puusepän
tekemässä arkussa, suvussani on ollut puuseppiä ja sanas-
sa on puu ja seppä, puu on tammi ja seppä Ilmarinen joka
takoi itselleen kultaisen naisen ja kultainen nainen oli
myös äitini.

by Tyne Saastamoinen

I live my silent words as I live my silent days—slowly I climb
the hillside or descend its slope; or I remain rooted like a marker
or a cairn, placed as a sign to passerby—these poems which
I eat and drink and sell, these are my own, like the nails on my
fingers and the nails on my feet, or they fall from my head like
hairs lost to brushing, grey as they have begun to be—but, I can
still knot a red ribbon in my hair, just for my pleasure, and when
I die, I hope to be like Hölderlin, with a crown on my head
wrought by a carpenter, that forger of wood, and laid in a coffin
he's made—in my family there were *puuseppiä*, and knotted in
this word is both the tree and the smithy: the tree is of oak and
the forger is Ilmarinen, who made for his pleasure a woman
from gold, and from gold emerged also my mother.

tr. Ellen Hinsey and
Heini Vartia-Delafont

ARCANES 6

Jean-Claude Renard

Comme reprise par les temps anciens
(ou saisie des puissances du corps)
l'oreille lit
— déchiffre sans *loas** l'écriture.
Et non moins qu'elle, par même secret, les pieds nus
posés sur le livre.
L'inévitable s'intensifie: fait un avec l'offrande.
Puis les yeux,
dans l'épaisseur du miroir,
voient un cri.
A chaque mort, nulle part et partout, débute quelque
chose.
Mais comment atteindre le hors-lieu,
trouver le vrai sens sous les filigranes,
la connivence:
— le mot de passe?

---

* Petits dieux haïtiens.

ARCANES 6

by Jean-Claude Renard

As though taken back by ancient times
(or seized by the body's powers)
the ear reads
— deciphers writing, without *loas*.[†]
And not less than the ear, by the same secret, bare feet
placed on the book.
The inevitable intensifies: becomes one with the offering.
Then the eyes,
in the thickness of the mirror,
see a cry.
At each death, nowhere and everywhere, something
begins.
But how can one reach outside of place,
find the true meaning under the watermarks,
the complicity:
the password?

tr. Catharine Savage Brosman

Minor Haitian gods.

ARCANES 7

Jean-Claude Renard

Comme une bouche absente
sans absence
le *non-né* profère dans le vide
le naître et le renaître.

Franchis
l'extérieur et l'intérieur,
savoir
ne sert plus à savoir.

Ce seul: ce sel
— ce *là-bas* plus proche que l'ici
fait en moi,
fait avec moi ses noces.

Présent partout et nulle part
l'*Un* (devenant ce qu'il n'est pas)
se multiplie
puis se rejoint dans l'Un.

Le silence
traverse le silence.

ARCANES 7

by Jean-Claude Renard

Like a mouth absent
without absence
the *non-born* utters, in emptiness,
the act of being born, and not being born.

Once the exterior and interior
have been crossed,
knowing
no longer serves for knowing.

This singleness: this salt
— this *over there* closer than here
creates in me,
creates with me its wedding.

Present everywhere and nowhere
the *One* (becoming what it is not)
multiplies itself,
then joins itself again in the One.

Silence
crosses through silence.

tr. Catharine Savage Brosman

ARCANES 8

Jean-Claude Renard

Être est exode
— comme l'apparence.
Derrière le sang
la négation naît de nous.

Toute espérance perdue
ne demeurent que démence et mort.
Autour des ruines
même l'absence ne parle plus.

Qu'aucune clôture n'exclue l'incertitude:
la fécondation nocturne!

Il est bon que n'en finisse pas
le partage fertile du feu.

ARCANES 8

by Jean-Claude Renard

Being is an exodus
— like appearance.
Behind blood
negation is born from us.

When all hope has been lost,
there remain only dementia and death.
Around the ruins
even absence no longer speaks.

Let no enclosure exclude uncertainty:
nocturnal richness!

It is good that the fertile sharing
of fire never end.

tr. Catharine Savage Brosman

ARCANES 9

Jean-Claude Renard

Avant tout nom: l'être.
Nommé,
il s'efface
— comme l'étier dans le sable.

Pistes perdues? Non.
Mais, dans l'interstice,
l'intime parole
sans livre.

A l'orée
de l'autre versant,
les tarots brûlent
— et le meurtre.

Rien n'est identique.
L'eau sauvée,
saurai-je parmi les racines
si la mort est inévitable?

ARCANES 9

by Jean-Claude Renard

Before every name: being.
Once named,
it is erased,
like the rivulet
in the sand.

Lost tracks? No.
But, in the crack,
the intimate word
without books.

At the very edge
of the other slope,
the tarots burn
— and murder.

Nothing is identical.
Water once saved,
will I know among the roots
if death is inevitable?

tr. Catharine Savage Brosman

RITES 6

Jean-Claude Renard

Devant la mer
qu'habite l'autre légende,
des femmes attirent les oiseaux.
Comment la parole,
par lèvres aveugles,
exorcise-t-elle
ces phrases fracturées de froid?
Un venin suinte des blessures,
ronge les mots, les exsangue
— givre le sens invisible...
Mais aux sources,
parmi les galets où l'énigme inscrit ses merveilles,
patiente l'enchantement.

RITES 6

by Jean-Claude Renard

Facing the sea
which the other legend inhabits,
women attract the birds.
How do words,
by blind lips,
exorcise
these fractured phrases of the cold?
Venom seeps from the wounds,
gnaws the dead, drains their blood
— frosts the invisible meaning...
But at the springs,
among the pebbles where the enigma writes its marvels,
enchantment bides its time.

tr. Catharine Savage Brosman

RITES 7

Jean-Claude Renard

Sous le pin-marabout (qui protège du mauvais œil),
ôte ta ceinture de laine rouge
puis, tatouée entre les sourcils,
invoque l'oiseau des hauts-lieux.
La cruche d'eau pure (pluie: poupée et pilon) t'a
marqué l'épaule.
Il y a des pays sans oranges ni roses,
mais la clématite coupée remonte toujours autour de l'arbre.
Toi, maintenant, nue dans les saules bleus,
refaite vierge par l'alun, l'écorce, la résine,
ah! belle comme le guêpier
— enduis de beurre le linteau de la porte
(à chaque serrure sa clé de bois)
et dehors, aux angles des terrasses, pose les marmites
de terre noire.
Bénites la pierre et la main près du genévrier
thurifère,
bois la liqueur de fleur de garance
et comme la «Négresse du Prophète», oreilles
peintes de henné,
fonde (par vertu du grain moulu avant l'aube)
fécondité dans l'ombre, fécondité dans la lumière.
Ceux d'en haut, ceux d'en bas
(avec, dans la peau de chèvre, les figues sèches et
l'orge grillée)
sont-ils,
des jours de la fronde et du javelot,
ces menhirs, encore debout, là, comme des lauriers-
roses géants entre les parois des ravins?

RITES 7

by Jean-Claude Renard

Under the marabout-pine (which protects against the evil eye),
remove your girdle of red wool
then, tattooed between your eyebrows,
invoke the bird of high places.
The pitcher of pure water (rain: poppet and pestle) has marked
your shoulder.
There are countries without oranges and roses,
but clematis cut down always climbs again around the tree.
You, naked now in the blue willows,
made virgin again through alum, bark, resin,
— ah! beautiful as the wasps' nest
coat the lintel of the door with butter
(for each keyhole its wooden key)
and outside, at the angles of the terraces, place dark earthen
jars.
Once blessed the stone and the hand near the incense-bearing
juniper tree,
drink the liquor of the madder plant,
and like the "Negress of the Prophet," ears painted with
henna,
found (by virtue of the grain ground before dawn)
fertility in shadow, fertility in light.
Are those from above, those from below
(with, in a goatskin, the dried figs and roasted barley),
— are they,
the days of slingshot and of javelin,
those menhirs, standing still, like great crepe myrtles
between the ravine walls?

tr. Catharine Savage Brosman

RITES 8

Jean-Claude Renard

Sache-le:
jamais tout n'est dit.
Car la langue n'ayant pas de fin
les mêmes mots faits neufs par chaque regard nu,
chaque unicité, chaque énigme
— parlent chaque fois autrement.
C'est pourquoi,
là,
dans le vertige de l'enfance,
d'indéchiffrables neiges imprègnent l'écriture.

RITES 8

by Jean-Claude Renard

Know this:
never is everything said.
For language having no end,
the same words made new by each naked glance,
each uniqueness, each enigma
— speak each time differently.
That is why,
there,
in the vertigo of childhood
writing is impressed by indecipherable snows.

tr. Catharine Savage Brosman

RITES 9

Jean-Claude Renard

La mort
mesure-t-elle l'amour?
L'amour
mesure-t-il la mort?

Nul ne le sait.

Mais l'âme rit
si, dans l'un et l'autre,
habite
l'abîme blanc du mystère.

RITES 9

by Jean-Claude Renard

Does death
measure love?
Does love
measure death?

No one knows.

But the soul laughs
if, in the one and the other,
there lives
the white abyss of mystery.

tr. Catharine Savage Brosman

SYLVE FLORENTINE

Quentin Ben Mongaryas

Quand tu es dans mes bras
Et que tu m'enivres des parfums
Du jardin fleuri de ton corps
Réceptacle vivant
Des cieux et des enfers
Mon cœur vrombit
Pivote se désintègre

Mon âme contemple
Dans tes yeux placides
Profondeurs nacrées
Aux mille arcs-en-ciel
Des appels envoûtants
Pour l'union des corps
Et mon cœur galope
Frémit se dilate

Prends mon amour
Les envols obligatoires
Des sens explosés
Où mon cœur tourbillonne

FLORENTINE WOODS

by Quentin Ben Mongaryas

When you are in my arms
You intoxicate me with the scents
Of the floral garden of your being
A living receptacle
Of the heavens and of hell
My heart buzzes
Turns crumbles

My soul contemplates
In your placid eyes
Profound pearly depths
Of a thousand rainbows
The bewitching call
For the union of two bodies
And my heart gallops
Vibrates expands

Take my love
This necessary journey
Of explosive senses
Where my heart is a whirlwind

tr. Stephanie Yang

ÄNGSTLICH

Annemarie Zornack

nun steige ich schon jahrelang
aus dem eisenbahncoupé
und habe den kindermantel
mit den kirschknöpfen an
ihr habt mich wohl
nicht wiedererkannt
jahrelang steige ich schon
bißchen ängstlich bißchen
erwartungsvoll habt ihr mich?
langsam werde ich
mir selber fremd bin nur
ein kinderfoto das vergilbt

ANXIOUS

by Annemarie Zornack

for year i've been climbing
down from the train
and have a child's coat on
with cherry buttons
you probably didn't
recognize me
for years i've been climbing
a little anxious a little
expectant do you have me?
slowly i'm becoming
a stranger even to me i'm only
a child's photo turning yellow

tr. Suzanne Shipley

MEINE KINDHEIT WAR EIN FRAGEZEICHEN

Annemarie Zornack

meine kindheit war ein fragezeichen
ich befragte die geschwungene
sofalehne das krumme ofenrohr
die gebogene kaffeekannentülle
die dickbauchige vase

die dinge gaben keine antwort
sie waren tanten onkel cousinen
beste freundinnen doch
sie gaben keine antwort

dabei hatte ich für uns alle
eine geheimsprache ausgedacht
zu der ich noch eine geheimschrift
erfand in der ließ sich
nichts sagen

MY CHILDHOOD WAS A QUESTION MARK

by Annemarie Zornack

my childhood was a question mark
i questioned the sprung
recliner the crooked stove-pipe
the bent coffee canister
the pear-shaped vase

the objects gave no answer
they were aunts uncles cousins
best friends yet
they gave no answer

for us all i thought up
a secret language
and to match it invented
a secret script for saying
nothing at all

tr. Suzanne Shipley

Annemarie Zornack
Germany

Lionello Grifo
Italy

FIGLI

Lionello Grifo

Lembi di carne
perduti
nell'impietoso oceano
della vita
che tutto travolge
di schianto...
senza misericordia
per il pianto
delle madri,
silènte.

CHILDREN

by Lionello Grifo

Shreds of flesh
lost
in the pitiless ocean
of life
that sweeps everything away
with no mercy
for the silent weeping
of the mothers.

tr. Marilena Tamburello

L'ULTIMO VINTO

Lionello Grifo

Si trascinò sui gomiti
fuori della sua grotta
e mi gridò veemente:

«Dove fuggirono i poeti,
quando il sangue dei vinti
macchiò i marciapiedi?»

THE LAST VANQUISHED

by Lionello Grifo

He dragged himself on his elbows
out of his cave
and shouted at me vehemently:

"Where did the poets flee,
when the blood of the vanquished
stained the sidewalks?"

tr. Marilena Tamburello

COME UNA VERGOGNA

Lionello Grifo

E' soprattutto di giorno
che vivace si mostra
nei Caffè
la solitudine di gruppo
delle anziane signore
dei paesi più agiati...

Ed è di notte, invece,
e silenziosa,
che ovunque sulla Terra,
si cela
come una vergogna
la solitudine
degli uomini soli!

LIKE A DISGRACE

by Lionello Grifo

It is mostly in the daytime
in the café
where the solitude of wealthy
older women
plays the lively game...

And it is in the nighttime
instead,
silently,
everywhere on earth,
that the solitude
of lonely men
hides
like a disgrace!

tr. Marilena Tamburello

UNA VISIONE DEL MEDITERRANEO

Lionello Grifo

...Come antica, ispirata melopèa
affioravan dall'acqua
parole mie d'un tempo
. . . . . .

...perché é lento, omotermico e profondo
come il grembo materno,
perché ivi conserva
le piú belle vestigia
di templi e monumenti
e totto quanto d'armonioso e grande
l'architettura dell'Uomo
abbia realizzato mai,

perché nessun'altra regione del globo
ha collezionato ed esposto al mondo
—pour le plaisir des yeux—
come ancor oggi dice
il bèrbero mercante,
quella dovizie di capolavori
che sono le cittá sorte ed affacciate
sulle sue rive inondate di sole...

perché incontro a lui
protende le lunghe braccia il delta
del grande fiume egizio
simbolo della sorgente della vita...

A VISION OF THE MEDITERRANEAN

by Lionello Grifo

...As an ancient inpired melopoeia
my forgone words
surfaced from the water

. . . . . .

...because this sea is slow,
homothermous and deep
as the maternal womb,
because it preserves
the most beautiful ruins
of temples and monuments
and all the grand and harmonious
architecture ever built by Man

because no other region in the world
collected and exhibited for everybody
—pour le plaisir des yeux—
as the Berber merchant
still says today,
that abundance of masterpieces
which are the cities built along its sun filled
shores...

because towards him
the delta of the wide Egyptian river
symbol of life's source
stretches out its long arms...

perché fu culla di ogni religione
ivi compresa quella delle Stelle
che permisero ai Magi
di annunciare agli uomini
la nascita di Cristo...

perché sulle sue terre
da Càdice a Smirne
nacque il pane, dono di Cèrere
dea della fertilitá e dell'abbondanza,
e prosperarono la vigna e l'ulivo
e il miele coló copiosissimo
sulla mandorla, sul dattero, sul fico,
sull'uva passa e il cedro,
e, tutto, amalgamato a latte
sidro e farina,
venne adagiato su foglie oliate
d'alloro romano e, cotto al forno,
si chiamó "placenta"!...

because it was the crib of every faith
including that of the Stars
which allowed the three kings
to announce to Man
the birth of Christ

because on its lands
from Cadiz to Ismir
bread, the gift of Ceres,
goddess of fertility and abundance
was invented,
and the wine and the olive thrived,
and honey dripped abundantly
on the almond, on the date, on the fig
on the raisin and on the citron
and all mixed with milk
cider and flour
was spread out on oiled laurel leaves
and cooked in the oven,
was called "placenta"!

tr. Marilena Tamburello

ED É ANCORA GUERRA

Lionello Grifo

...E che cos'è Poesia
se non un canto
che si leva
antico e sempre nuovo
sulle antiche sciagure
e sempre nuovo
dell'umanità?!

WAR STILL GOES ON

by Lionello Grifo

...What is poetry
but an ancient dream and forever new
song
that soars
on the ancient and forever new
disasters of humanity?!

tr. Marilena Tamburello

JE SUIS UN NÈGRE

Charles Nokan

Je suis un nègre.
J'étais esclave sous César.
J'ai bâti les pyramides, les châteaux et les gratte-ciel.
Je suis noir comme une nuit sans lune.
Mon sang a fertilisé les plaines de l'égoïste Europe.
J'ai trimé dans les plantations,
les usines des colons et des Yankees.
Je suis un nègre qui se souviendra toujours de ses
        multiples chaînes.

Je souffre au Congo.
Au Mozambique, en Angola,
les balles du colonialisme et de l'impérialisme
ont brisé mon crâne et déchiré mon cœur.
Je suis le prolétaire tombé devant son taudis à Saint-Domingue,
en Algérie et au Viet-Nam...
Je suis un noir fier qui dresse ses poings
contre toute oppression.
Je suis Toussaint Louverture, Lumumba, Ben Barka.

I AM A NEGRO

by Charles Nokan

I am a negro
I was a slave under Caesar
I built the pyramids, the castles and the skyscrapers
I am as black as a moonless night
My blood has fertilized the fields of a self-absorbed Europe
I exhausted myself on the plantations
in the factories of the colonists and the Yankees
I am a negro who will forever remember his many bondages

I suffer in the Congo
in Mozambique, in Angola
The bullets of colonialism and imperialism
have cracked my skull and have torn apart my soul
I am the working man fallen in front of his slum in St. Domingue
in Algeria and in Vietnam
I am a proud black man with fists ready to fight
against all oppression
I am Toussaint Louverture, Lumumba, Ben Barka

tr. Stephanie Yang

종점

정정선

출발하겠어요.
여기는 종점이에요.

차를 타시면
제 좌석에 앉으셔야죠.

산에는 나무
강에는 고기.

여러분, 시계를 보고 계세요
타고 내리실 정거장 기억하세요.

길이란 옷깃을 스치기 마련이구요.
천년 인연도 스치기만 한데요.

제 그림자는 밟으셔도 좋아요.
팔만사천 보따리만 챙겨가시면.

직행이든
완행이든.

허어엄, 여러분을 모시는 종점까지는
제가 운전수.

여기는 종점이에요.
출발하겠어요.

WAYSIDE STATION

by Sunny Jung

I start to leave
at the end.

A passenger
in the given seat.

A tree in the mountain,
a fish in the river.

Check the time
of your departure and arrival.

Whose sleeve you touch
has a one thousand year bond.

You can step on my shadow,
if you take eighty four thousand of your belongings.

Choose direct
or detour.

No, no. Until the last stop
I am the driver.

Here is the end
and the beginning.

tr. Elizabeth Bartlett
and Sunny Jung

그릇

오세영

깨진 그릇은
칼날이 된다.

節制와 均衡의 중심에서
빗나간 힘,
부서진 원은 모를 세우고
理性의 차가운 눈을 뜨게 한다.

盲目의 사랑을 노리는
사금파리여,
지금 나는 맨발이다.
베어지기를 기다리는
살이다.
상처 깊숙히서 성숙하는 魂.

깨진 그릇은
칼날이 된다.
무엇이나 깨진 것은
칼이 된다.

A BOWL

by Se-young Oh

A broken bowl
    becomes the blade of a knife.

The broken circle becomes a blade
    opening the cold eyes of reason.
Energy glances off
    the center of moderation and balance.

Fragment of the broken bowl
    that aims blind love,
I am now barefoot,
    the flesh
    waiting to be cut.
A soul maturing in the deep wound.

A broken bowl
    becomes the blade of a knife.
Any broken thing
    becomes a knife.

tr. Sunny Jung

靜寂

송수권

절門 밖에는 언제나 별들이 싱그러운 포도밭을 이루고 있었다.
빗장을 풀어놓은 낡은 절간 門 위에는 밤새도록 걸어온 달이
한 나그네처럼 기웃거리며 포도를 따고 있었다.
먹물처럼 떨어진 산봉우리들이 담비떼들같이 떠들며 모여들고
따다 흘린 포도 몇 알이 쭈루룩
山窓을 흘러가다 구슬 깨지는 소리를 내고 있었다.

SILENCE

by Soo-Kwan Song

Nightly, beyond the temple gate, stars formed new vines of grapes.
Above the worn and unlocked temple gate,
The moon, like a peaking vagabond,
Walked all night harvesting grapes.

Ink black mountain peaks gathered like a gaggling herd of marten
As a few harvested grapes that spilled forth
Glided across a mountain view window
Then crashed like breaking jade.

tr. Sunny Jung

KAILSALS

Vizma Belševica

Sasalis kā acs, kas uz savu mīlestību caur
    citu acīm paskatījusies, un vientuļš, ka
    ne niedres pūka neaizmetas, pāri skrienot:
                            tā ezers.

Sastingusi kā mute, kas — no citu vārdiem
    par savu mīlestību — mēma, ka ne
    dvašas dūniņas pār lūpām:
                            tā es.

Šķirti kā egļu gali — šis uz debesīm, tas
    uz dzelmi, bet saknes, saknes taču vienas:
                            tā laikam mēs.
Bet tevis te nav. Un es nevaru paraudāt.

BLACK FROST

by Vizma Belševica

Frozen like an eye that's looked at its love through
    the eyes of others, and lonely, so not even
    the fluff of a reed catches as it races across:
                    that's the lake.

Grown numb like a mouth so thoroughly silenced by others'
    words about its love that not a down
    of breath crosses its lips:
                    that's me.

Separated, two spruces — one pointing skyward, one
    toward the deep, though the roots,
    the roots are really the same:
                    that must be us.
But you aren't here. And I can't have a cry.

tr. Ilze Kļaviņa Mueller

SVĒTĪGI IR TIE GARĀ VĀJIE

Vizma Belševica

Svētīgi ir tie garā vājie,
Kā vakara pļavas miglotiem prātiem,
Jo viņiem pieder debesu valstība
Savu vājumu neapzināties.
Tu sakies stipra. Tad esi līdz galam,
Un nav ko melot, ka dievs tevi dzinis.
Kopš sāki atšķirt labu no ļauna,
Nav paradīzes. Tu vienkārši — zini.
Un prāta tuksnesī akmeņainā
Tev tagad jāpūlas vaiga sviedros
Ieaudzēt mazu ilūziju.
Kādu gaisīgi trauslu ticības ziedu.
Turēt ap pumpuru plaukstu un elpas
Nedrošo aizvēju ledainā smieklā
Un laimīgai būt to īso brīdi,
Uz kuru izdosies sevi piekrāpt.

BLESSED ARE THE POOR IN SPIRIT

by Vizma Belševica

Blessed are the poor in spirit,
Their minds misty like evening meadows,
For theirs is the kingdom of heaven
Of not realizing their weakness.
You claim to be strong. Then go all the way,
Don't lie that it was God who drove you.
Ever since you began to tell right from wrong,
There's been no paradise. You simply—know.
And in the stony desert of the mind
You must now labor in the sweat of your brow
To grow a small illusion.
Some airily fragile blossom of faith.
Hold your palm around the bud, around your breath's
Precarious lee in an icy laugh,
Be happy for the short moment
You manage to fool yourself.

tr. Ilze Kļaviņa Mueller

JURĢĪNES IZPRECINĀŠANA

Vizma Belševica

Nu paskat', cik labi — nevajag
Ne sava prāta,
Ne sava kāta.
Pie mieta piesieta jurģīne
Ir droša un pasargāta.
Ne lauzta, ne dubļos iepērta,
Spīd viņas zeltsārtā saulība.
Ir taču laimīga ļoti — vai ne? —
Tāda mieta
Un zieda
Laulība.

THE DAHLIA'S MARRIAGE

by Vizma Belševica

Well, isn't this nice — no need
for a mind of your own
or a stalk of your own.
A dahlia tied to a stake
is safe and protected.
Neither broken nor
crushed in the mud,
its golden-red sunny face
is radiant.
Such a perfect match,
don't you think? This
marriage between
the stake and
the flower.

tr. Ilze Kļaviņa Mueller

NEBRĒC UZ LIEPU, VIŅA ZIEDĒS

Vizma Belševica

Nebrēc uz liepu, viņa ziedēs, kad būs viņas laiks.
Patīk — skaties uz viņas ziediem. Nepatīk — neskaties.
Tas ir viss, ko tu vari darīt.

Un protams — nocirst liepu tu vari jebkurā brīdī.
Dari to droši.
Zieda un cirvja strīdā uzvarētājs vienmēr būs cirvis.
Pēc tam neaizmirsti noslaucīt zābakus viņas ziedos:
Nekāds pasaules zīds nav maigāks par liepziedu drīksnām.
Un nebaidies no tām zemē notriektajām bitēm.
Par mēģinājumu iedzelt zābakā
Bite maksā ar dzīvību.

DON'T SCREAM AT THE LINDEN TREE

by Vizma Belševica

Don't scream at the linden tree, it will bloom in its own season.
If you like, look at its blossoms. If not, don't look.
That is all you can do.

And—it goes without saying—you can chop down the linden
whenever you please.
Go right ahead.
In a dispute between blossom and axe the axe will win every time.
When you're done, don't forget to wipe your boots on its flowers:
There is no silk in the world softer than linden blossoms.
And don't be afraid of the bees that were dashed to the ground.
For trying to sting a boot
The bee pays with its life.

tr. Ilze Kļaviņa Mueller

ES JAU NEGRIBU DAUDZ

Vizma Belševica

Es jau negribu daudz.
Tādu sīkumu.
Neiespējamo.
Lai tās vizbules rudās
Ar drūpošām drīksnām
Izkāpj no grāmatas,
Zemē un aprīļa vējā
Ieaug atpakaļ zilas
Un māllēpes divas zem blīgznām
(Kā zem pelēkās debess
Mēs abi tai mēmajā spriegumā)
Kļūst par atskaites punktiem,
Lai sākam
No šīs vietas par jaunu.
Kausējam ledu un sniegu
No savu siržu ziemas.
Panākam nepanākamo,
Aizskrējušo —
Kā upe zem ļodzīgā tiltiņa,
Izkaisīto —
Kā pūpola putekšņi vējā,
Notveram plaukstās,
Un vainīgās elpās sildīt:
Mūsu divatu.
Vizbules.
Sīkumu.
Neiespējamo.

I'M REALLY NOT ASKING FOR MUCH

by Vizma Belševica

I'm really not asking for much.
Just a trifle.
The impossible.
I want those rust hepaticas
With their crumbling stigmas
To step out of the book,
To grow back, blue once more,
Into the soil and the April wind.
I want the two coltsfoots under the willows
(Like the two of us
Under gray skies in mute tension)
To become items
In the balancing of our account
So we can start
Over again from this point on.
Let's melt the ice and snow
From our hearts' winter.
Let's overtake what can't be overtaken,
What has sped by—
Like the creek under the tottery bridge.
Let's catch what's been scattered—
Like pussywillow pollen in the breeze,
In our palms, and warm it in our
Guilty breaths:
This twosome of ours.
Hepaticas.
A trifle.
The impossible.

tr. Ilze Kļaviņa Mueller

OZOLI

Vizma Belševica

I.

Kad, raugoties uz ceriņpumpuriem,
Tik kaili neaizsargātiem, tik gaiši zaļiem,
Sirds šķita žēlabās un izmisumā plīstam
Kā lauska sperta ābele; kad likās —
Ar kailu krūti jāmetas pret sniegu
Un jākausē, un jāglābj krūšu tiesa,
Ja vairāk nevar —
              pasmaidīja ziema.
Kā mātes smaids par bērna neprātību
Pa sniegiem dzirkstis pārskrēja, un maigi
Man sniegi pavērās, un ziema teica:
—Skaties!

II.

Neviens to nezina, ka ozols visupirms
Ir roze. Zīles cietais pumpurs šķeļas
Ap sārtāk, sārtāk satvīkstošu ziedu,
Un ilgi roze deg zem saltā sniega,
Līdz šaujas asnos sarkanos, un nav
Starp rozēm raženām, kas dvīņus nenestu,
Un nav starp rozēm raženām, kas bītos —

OAKS

by Vizma Belševica

I.

When, looking at the lilac buds,
So bare and unprotected, so bright green,
It seemed my heart would burst with sorrow and despair
Like an apple tree when the frost cracks it;
When it seemed I must throw myself, bare-breasted,
Upon the snow, and melt it, and save the part
My breast could warm, if that was all
I could do —
                                    winter suddenly smiled.
Like a mother's smile at her child's foolishness,
Sparks ran across the snowdrifts, and gently
The snows opened for me, and winter said:
— Look!

II.

Nobody knows that at first the oak
Is a rose. The acorn's hard bud splits
Around a blossom that glows redder,
Ever redder, and for a long time
The rose keeps burning under the cold snow
Until it surges into coral red shoots:
There's not a single fecund rose that doesn't
Bear twins, not one that fears —

III.

To nāvi mežakuiļa zobos šņakstošos,
To rožu nāvi — tomēr mežakuiļa,
Ne žļebīgajā mutē mājas cūkai,
Ko balti ļumīgu pēc sava ģīmja
Un līdzības ir cilvēks radījis,
To nāvi sīļa knābī, sārti nospuldzot
Pret zilu spārnu un pret baltu sniegu,
To nāvi zobos vāverei — bet plauks
Un plauks zem sniega rozes —
Dzemdēt ozolus.
Un, ja ies bojā pēdējā, tad citu,
Tad nākošgadu plauks, bet viņam jādzimst,
Tam ozolam.

IV.

Sniegs aizveras, un atkal balti klaji...

III.

That death between the chomping teeth
Of a wild boar, a rose's death—and still,
Death at a wild boar's teeth, not
At the slurping snout of a domestic pig,
Created by man in his own likeness,
Like his own visage, flabby, white;
Or death in a jay's beak, a flash of red
Against a blue wing and against white snow;
Or death in a squirrel's teeth—yet roses
Will keep on budding, budding under snow —
And then give birth to oaks.
And should the last rose perish,
Another will bud next year,
But the oak —
Must be born.

IV.

The snow closes, and again the plain is white...

tr. Ilze Kļaviņa Mueller

MIERS VIRS ZEMES

Vizma Belševica

Pār zaļiem laukiem rudens miglas maigums.
Ne tālumu. Ne debess. Melni koki
Raud baltām asarām. Stāv nolāsojis zars
Kā laimi sagaidījis — mēmā mirdzējumā,
Un putni — blīvi pumpuri — tai zarā
Uz lidojumu neplaukst, aizmirsuši
Par salkumu, par visām putnu raizēm,
Un pati aizmirsusi. Āpkārt lēnums tāds,
Ka liekas:

      miers virs zemes,
      cilvēkiem labs prāts.

PEACE ON EARTH

by Vizma Belševica

Over green fields the gentleness of autumn fog.
No distances. No sky. Black trees
Weeping white tears. A branch covered with drops of water stands
Like one who has awaited happiness — in a mute glow,
And birds — dense buds — on that branch
Do not open into flight, having forgotten
About hunger, about all that worries birds,
And I too have forgotten. Around me is such slowness
That it seems:

> peace on earth
> goodwill to all.

tr. Ilze Kļaviņa Mueller

DZIESMAS GAIDĪŠANA

Vizma Belševica

jo pavasaris sākas tad
kad grāvjos brūnas vardes sēž
      un kaut ko gaida
un saules piemirdzētais ūdens
dzintarainu kūlu skalo
un kūlā zaļi asni vīd
      un vardes gaida
to lielo dziedāšanas stundu
no gavilēm kad ūdens virmos
un visi grāvji cilāsies
      no varžu dziesmām
bet tālu vēl
līdz skaustu krumšļiem
brūnas vardes grāvjos sēž
un lāgiem paver zelta acis
zelta saulē paskatās
      un dziesmu gaida

WAITING FOR SONG

by Vizma Belševica

for spring begins
when in the ditches brown frogs sit
           and wait for something
and water, filled with glints of sun,
laps over last year's amber grass
and in the grass green shoots appear
           and the frogs wait
for that great hour of singing
when the water
vibrates with exultation
and all the ditches heave
           with the frogs' songs
but that's still far away
up to their knobby napes
brown frogs sit in the ditches
from time to time flick open golden eyes
look at the golden sun
           and wait for song

tr. Ilze Kļaviņa Mueller

A GRAPHIC WITH A SPECIMEN OF MAN
FROM THE BRONZE AGE

by Katica Ćulavkova

In the archeological museum in Celje
lies a man, a trunk
with all characteristics of a graphic

in gray shades of Istrian stone
like cement, like a spider's web
like a city's periphery
like a wig for the elderly

with bones placed so
that horror, not sorrow, penetrates you
with a hated message

that only needs to be transferred onto paper
imprinted carefully in a small edition
and be sent to admirers
of art and life.

Isn't man sometimes beautiful?

tr. Dasha Čulić Nisula

THE NECK — NEURALGIC PLACES

by Katica Ćulavkova

The neck — entrance to Mycenae
(not all graves are public)
out of the sediment unconsciousness—history
turns there forward and backward
the trade of valuable objects
art — not — for art's sake:
the twentieth century suddenly together!

A general bewilderment is not enough
to change the shape of a woman
and the challenge of her neck

      "In some cases
      the archetype is harmful for..." or
      "The cult is organic matter —
      it is not lost, it is transformed," etc.

news that delights:
youthfulness of shape (Modigliani)
harbinger of newly discovered beauty
(and Tsvetaeva's invisible fingers
at the occiput of the long heavy winter)
mimicry of hidden protest
all in all
the anti-grammar of despair

— know thyself
and more (neck associations)
a passage that pulsates — oppressed hope
a cliff in which contrabass reasounds
and male Argonauts
from other worlds
do not abandon the search:
entrace into a woman is infinitely long

let your will be free!

tr. Dasha Čulić Nisula

EGOÍSMO

Gloria de Sant'Anna

Eu,
estudar apenas
o sentido estético da tarde.

Nem grandes sentimentos,
rolando
em alinhamentos compactos
das reminiscências
dos factos, ou não.

Nunca atitudes suspensas,
vindas de conhecimentos
vastos,
da grande multidão das coisas
com sequência.

Nada.

Apenas eu, estudando
através do gozo de estar ao sol
numa cadeira vermelha
já velha,
o sentido estético da tarde.

EGOISM

by Gloria de Sant'Anna

Here I am
merely studying
the aesthetic meaning of the afternoon.

No great sentiments,
rolling
in compact alignment
of remembered
facts, or not.

No suspended expressions,
coming from vast stores
of information,
about a great multitude of things
sequential.

Nothing.

Only me, studying
the aesthetic meaning of the afternoon
through the pleasure of sitting in the sun
on a red chair
already gone old.

tr. Ivana Rangel-Carlsen

PRIMEIRO POEMA DO NEGRINHO MORTO

Gloria de Sant'Anna

O negrinho é morto
na noite densa.
(Quem lhe segreda é o vento.)

Morto e quieto
no seu esquife.
(Quem o abraça são as reízes.)

Já nada o prende
nada o magoa.
(Quem o lementa é a chuva.)

De tão sozinho
de tão ausente,
quem o redime é o tempo.

FIRST POEM OF THE DEAD LITTLE BLACK BOY

by Gloria de Sant'Anna

The little black boy is dead
in the thick night.
(The wind whispers to him.)

Dead and silent
in his coffin.
(The roots will embrace him.)

Nothing holds him any longer
nothing can hurt him.
(The rain mourns him.)

So alone
so absent,
only time can redeem him.

tr. Ivana Rangel-Carlsen

MATERNIDADE

Gloria de Sant'Anna

Olho-te: és negra.
Olhas-me: sou branca.
Mas sorrimos as duas
na tarde que se adeanta.

Tu sabes e eu sei:
o que ergue altivamente o meu vestido
e o que soergue a tua capulana,
é a mesma carga humana

Quando soar a hora
determinada, crua, dolorosa
de conceder ao mundo o mistério da vida,

seremos tão iguais, tão verdadeiras,
tão míseras, tão fortes
E tão perto da morte...

que este sorriso de hoje,
na tarde que se esvai,
é o testemunho exacto
do erro das fronteiras raciais.

Dos nossos ventres altos,
os filhos que brotarem
nos chamarão com a mesma palavra.

E ambas estamos certas
—tu, negra e eu, branca—
que é dentro dos nossos ventres
que germina a esperança.

MOTHERHOOD

by Gloria de Sant'Anna

I look at you: you're black
You look at me: I'm white.
But we smile together
in the waning afternoon.

You know and I know:
that what proudly raises my dress
and what partially lifts your *capulana*
is the same human freight we carry.

When the time comes
the predetermined, raw, painful time
of bringing out the mystery of life to the world

we shall be so alike, so real,
so miserable, so strong
and so close to death...

that our smile today,
in the waning afternoon
is an unequivocal demonstration
of the mistake of racial separation.

The children springing
from our raised bellies
shall call us by the same word.

And we are both certain
—you, black, and I, white—
that it's inside our wombs
that hope germinates.

tr. Ivana Rangel-Carlsen

157

POEMA PARA UM DIA DE CHUVA

Gloria de Sant'Anna

A minha casa é um farol no meio da noite

Vem, sejas quem fores

ficarás a princípio como a haste de uma flor
gotejando sobre o tapete

e nós olhar-te-emos
da cor da chuva

mas imediatamente, quase imediatamente
sentirás nas tuas as palmas quentes
das nossas mãos

e acharás no desenho dos nossos risos
a tradução de hora

POEM FOR A RAINY DAY

by Gloria de Sant'Anna

My house is a beacon in the middle of the night

Come, whoever you are

at first you shall stand
like the stem of a flower dripping on the rug

and we will see in you
the color of the rain

but immediately, or nearly so
you will feel the warm palms of our hands in yours

and you will find the essence of the moment
in the shape of our smiles

tr. Ivana Rangel-Carlsen

PARAGEM

Gloria de Sant'Anna

Não árvore,
não caibo nos teus braços.

Eu desci de um caminho mais distante
perdido na memória.

Deixai-me seguir só pela terra adeante,
que um dia voltarei vinda do mar.

Busca-me então desesperadamente,
ergue meu corpo esparso.
Eu cantarei saudades docemente
quando o vento surgir das noites de luar.

Deixar-me seguir só pela terra adeante
que um dia voltarei vinda do mar...

STOPPING PLACE

by Gloria de Sant'Anna

No, tree,
I don't fit in your arms.

I came down from a more distant road
lost in memory.

Let me go on alone through the earth,
and one day I shall return from the sea.

Search for me then desperately,
lift my meager body.
I shall sing my yearning sweetly
when the wind blows in moonlit nights.

Let me go on alone through the earth,
and one day I shall return from the sea.

tr. Ivana Rangel-Carlsen

A ARTE DOS VERSOS

Eugenio de Andrade

Toda a ciência está aqui,
na maneira como esta mulher
dos arredores de Cantão,
ou dos campos de Alpedrinha,
rega quatro ou cinco leiras
de couves: mão certeira
com a água,
intimidade com a terra,
empenho do coração.
Assim se faz o poema.

THE ART OF POETRY

by Eugenio de Andrade

All the art is here,
in the way this woman
from the outskirts of Canton
or the fields of Alpedrinha
waters her four or five rows
of cabbages: the sure hand,
intimacy with the earth,
the heart's commitment.
That's how a poem is made.

tr. Alexis Levitin

O REI DE ÍTACA

Sophia de Mello Breyner Andresen

A civilização em que estamos é tão errada que
Nela o pensamento se desligou da mão

Ulisses rei de Ítaca carpinteirou seu barco
E gabava-se também de saber conduzir
Num campo a direito o sulco do arado

THE KING OF ITHACA

by Sophia de Mello Breyner Andresen

So wrong the civilization in which we live that
In it thought has moved away from hand

Ulysses, King of Ithaca, carpentered his bark
And proud he was as well in knowing how to carve
Straight through a field the ploughshare's furrow.

tr. Alexis Levitin

SEMI-RIMBAUD

Sophia de Mello Breyner Andresen

Seu rosto é uma caverna
Onde frios ventos cantam

Passa rasgando o luar
E desesperando a noite

Pelas ruas oblíquas da cidade
Em madrugadas duvidosas
Constrói o mal com gestos cautelosos
E sonha a inversão total das coisas

Constrói o mal com gestos rigorosos
Lúcido de vício e de noitada
Íntegro como um poema
Completo lógico sem falha

A aurora desenha o seu rosto com os dedos
As suas órbitas iguais às das caveiras
Seu rosto voluntário e inventado
Magro de solidão verde de intensa
Vontade de negar e não ceder

De caminhar de mão dada com o nojo
De ser um espectro para terror dos vivos
E uma acusação escrita nas paredes

SEMI-RIMBAUD

by Sophia de Mello Breyner Andresen

His face is a cavern
Where cold winds sing

He passes shredding the moonlight
And driving the night to despair

Through the slant streets of the city
In doubtful dawns
He elaborates evil with careful gestures
And dreams the total inversion of things

He models evil with exacting gestures
Lucid from vice and the sleepless night
Integral as a poem
Complete logical flawless

The dawn draws his face with its fingers
His eye sockets like those of a skull
His face willed and invented
Thin from solitude, green from the intense
Desire to negate and not give in

To walk hand in hand with disgust
To be a specter for the terror of the living
And an accusation written on the walls

tr. Alexis Levitin

ESCREVO COMO UM ANIMAL...

Fiama Hasse Pais Brandão

Escrevo como um animal, mas com menor
perfeição alucinatória. Não sei imprimir as três linhas
convergentes do pé da gaivota, nem os pomos
leves da pata dos felinos. Só de uma forma rudimentar
escrevo, e estou a predestinar-me ao fim.
Depois de tantos séculos posso afirmar
que a escrita é uma escravidão dura.
Sei que é inútil e desumano mover as mãos
assim. Nem estou convicta de que seja digno
escrever desta maneira; é uma manufactura triste,
quando as mãos podiam apenas escarvar
na terra ou no corpo. Podem ficar as palavras
somente na fita magnética como nas cabeças loiras.
Nada na infância nos deveria obrigar
a traçar as patas dos roedores repelentes
que são letras. O som da boca deve escrever-se
no écran, com a nova razão da nova máquina
da realidade. Na areia, porém, ou no mosaico molhado
terei de aperfeiçoar a minha pegada. Aproximar
dela a mão até alcançar a harmonia do trilho
do escaravelho. Uma fieira de montículos
e ranhuras até ao infinito que para ele é o mar.

Há quantos séculos os seres humanos me aprisionaram
no mito da caligrafia. Como tem sido penoso esse gesto,
há tanto tempo, e só eu o renego, porque sinto
a opressão com que alguém o tornou mais nobre
do que a minha fala ou a minha visão, únicas
propensões inatas. Prefiro aprender pormenorizadamente

I WRITE LIKE AN ANIMAL...

by Fiama Hasse Pais Brandão

I write like an animal, but with less
hallucinatory perfection. I don't know how to leave the print of three
convergent lines on a sea gull's foot or the light
pads of feline. I can only write in a rudimentary
way, predestining myself to my end.
After so many centuries I can affirm
that writing is a hard enslavement.
I know that it is futile and inhuman to move my hands
like this. Nor am I convinced that it is dignified
to write this way; it's a sad handicraft,
when the hands can only scratch the surface
of the earth or of a body. Words could just as well
stay on a tape or inside blond heads.
Nothing in childhood should have forced us
to trace out those disgusting rodent paws,
the letters of the alphabet. The sound of the mouth ought to be written
on a screen, with the new reasoning of the new machine
of reality. It's in the sand, however, or on wet tiles
that I will have to hone my tracks. To extend
my hand toward it, till I reach the harmony of the
beetle's path. A row of tiny hillocks
and gulleys, leading to the infinite, which for it is the sea.

For how many centuries has humankind imprisoned me
in the myth of calligraphy! As if this gesture had turned to pain,
so long ago, and I alone renounce it, for I feel
the oppression with which someone has turned it more noble
than my speech or my seeing, my only
innate propensities. I'd rather learn in detail

a conservar uma impressão digital. Há um pensamento
abstracto e maquinal que decora a História com inteligência
mecânica, e por isso é supérfluo escrever. Só alguns
raros escribas, como os desenhadores de máquinas,
seriam necessários. E poderia descansar a cabeça
no regaço da lama.

Ensinaria à infância a gravar
no pó de talco a palma das mãos e a considerar as palavras
modulações da voz pura, sem a mancha embaciada
compacta que paira diante dos olhos sempre
que se fala. A mancha que se desloca no raio de visão
e disbota qualquer imagem como a chama de uma vela
com a fuligem constante a torná-la opaca.

how to preserve a fingerprint. There is an abstract
and mechanical thought that memorizes History with mechanical
intelligence, therefore it is superfluous to write. Only a few
rare scribes, like designers of machines,
would be needed. And I could rest my head
in a lap of mud.
                                        I would teach children to engrave
their palms in talcum powder and to consider words
modulations of pure voice, without that thick and tarnished
stain that hovers before one's eyes whenever
one speaks. A stain that moves within the field of vision
and smudges every image like the flame of a candle,
its endless soot turning it opaque.

tr. Alexis Levitin

CANTO DAS CHAMAS

Fiama Hasse Pais Brandão

Bendigo o Prometeu agrilhoado
que por mim sofreu os seus grilhões
e me trouxe as chamas de Paixão;
serena dor, a *solidão sonora.*
Na lareira estala e geme a lenha,
martírio doce meu de cada dia
que mais me salva a alma do que as artes
me salvam de cair na Dor diária.
Bendigo o martírio da Cruz viva
O signo do Sol amou-me em Agosto,
Aries cobriu o fogo com o velo
que eu vi na ficta infância desdobrar-se
da tesoura de Átropos, em figura
do meu velho Caseiro vivo e morto
que marcava na sazão o tempo certo
da tosquia, da poda, da cremação.
Amo as minhas achas de nogueira e vinha
recolhidas ainda no tempo de podar,
e sei que as chamas loquazes ardem
cada uma com o seu timbre e o seu compasso
para me lembrarem o canto dos seus nomes.

SONG OF THE FLAMES

by Fiama Hasse Pais Brandão

Blessed be Prometheus bound
who suffered in his chains for me
and brought me flames of Passion,
a quiet pain, *reverberating solitude.*
In the fireplace, the wood crackles and moans,
my sweet and daily martyrdom
that saves my soul more than the arts
save me from sinking into daily Pain.
Blessed be the martyr of the living Cross
who gave me in the evening these dark flames.
The sign of the Sun loved me in August,
Aries covered the fire with the fleece
I saw in fictive childhood droop back
from the scissors of Atropos, there in the shape
of my old Farm-hand alive and dead,
who marked the right time in the turning seasons
for sheep-shearing, pruning, and for burning.
I love my logs of walnut and thickened vineyard vine,
already gathered during pruning time,
and I know that the loquacious flames burn
each with its own timbre, its own beat,
to remind me of the song within their names.

tr. Alexis Levitin

IN MEMORIAM

Egito Goncalves

Um dia para ti confusa boca eu fui
na névoa de um comboio que afastava
a memória dos corpos. Clarões
intermitentes ofuscavam a janela
que a noite embaciava e entre carris
rasgava já uma dor que nem nascera.
Não sabíamos que afinal
na escrita
se perdia o rosto. Que buscá-lo
era lavrar o inverno, dispor
os ácidos, desalinhar o incenso. Quando
o gelo funde ainda lembro
resinas, esfarrapados nimbus,
uma pedra estriada que algum dia
fotografei para logo perder. O eco
repercute na folha de papel
que do título esperava certamente
uma elegia. Escondo-me
atrás de persianas que me escondem
as veredas onde poderia acaso
outra voz ter nascido.

IN MEMORIAM

by Egito Goncalves

One day, for you I was a confused mouth
in the fog of a train that was moving away from
the memory of our bodies. Flashes of light
obscured the window
tarnished by the night, and between the carriages
a pain was tearing open which hadn't yet been born.
We didn't know that in the end
the face would be lost
in the writing. That to search for it
would be to plough the winter, line up
acids, scatter disordered incense. When
the ice melts, I still remember
resin, loose drifting nimbus clouds,
a striped stone I photographed
one day only to lose it. The echo
reverberates on the sheet of paper,
which from its title surely awaits
an elegy. I hide
behind the Persian blinds that hide from me
those pathways where by chance
another voice might have had its birth.

tr. Alexis Levitin

CUNOȘTI TU ȚARA
UNDE ÎNFLORESC LĂMÂII?

Mircea Cărtărescu

aștept tramvaiul 26 în stație la circul de stat.
toată șoseaua e aurie, iar copacii verzi, verzi și cu atâtea frunze
că nici un renascentist nu le-ar putea picta pe toate.
mă holbez după tipe cu blugi și tricouri foarte largi
—pe țâțica uneia scrie JOGGING— mă sucesc, mă-nvârtesc
trece un cinci și pun degetul pe tabla lui roșie, caldă, și mă gândesc
          la un vers
îl și formulez: „în vara asta toți am devenit mecanici auto,
toți meșterim ceva pe sub caroseriile norilor"...

e jumătatea lui mai, e soare și sunt buimac
copiii aduc profesoarelor crăci grosolane de lilac
și lăcrămioare în celofan
dacă te uiți în soare rămâi în ochi cu un șpan
mov lunecos, iar pe retină
cu mutre și panglici violet de lumină.
soare, sticlosule, luno, hirsuto,
în vara asta toți am devenit un fel de mecanici auto,
toți meșterim ceva pe sub caroseriile norilor
toți deșurubăm axul cardanic al florilor.

în fine, după un șir de 24 și 4 apare și 26.
mă-nghesui și urc și-mi găsesc un loc lângă geamul din spate.

DO YOU KNOW THE COUNTRY
WHERE LEMON TREES BLOOM?

by Mircea Cărtărescu

I'm waiting for the no. 26 tram at the stop by the state circus.
the wide road looks golden and the trees are green, green
                                        and so full of leaves
that even a renaissance painter couldn't paint them all.
I'm staring at the girls in jeans and baggy T-shirts
—JOGGING I read across one's budding tits— I twist around,
                                        completely wheel about
a no. 5 passes by and I run my fingertips over the warm,
                        red steel plating, conceiving of a verse
and phrasing it: "this summer we've all become auto mechanics,
we're all repairing something under the clouds' body shop..."

it's the middle of may, it's summer and I'm becoming quite a wack
children bring their schoolteachers coarse branches of lilac
a cellophane-wrapped lily-of-the-valley
if you look at the sun you'll get jabbed in the eye
by slippery-mauve splinters, and on your retina
a glare of faces and violet ribbons with a bright patina.
you, o glassy sun, you moon, o hirsute body astronomic,
this summer we've all become a sort of auto mechanic,
we're all repairing something under the clouds' body shop
we're all unscrewing the flowers' axle shafts nonstop.

finally, after a series of 24's and 4's—a 26.
I push into the crowd and climb on, finding a place
                                        against the rear window.

şoseaua scânteiază de te înnebuneşte,
dar inima ta e rece, căci n-ai nici o dragoste
şi nu mai înţelegi nimic din vitrine
şi nu mai poţi scrie, decât scrisori tâmpite şi inutile.
deschid „trecutul utopic" de himmelmann cu frumoasa ei
                                        copertă albastră
şi citesc ce gândea goethe despre statui.

bucureştiul, la dreapta şi stânga, este şi nu-i.

the glitter of the street can make you feverish,
but your heart is cold, for you have no love
and in the shop windows you can't make out anything
and you can't write, only letters, dumb and useless.
I open himmelmann's *the utopian past* bound in beautiful blue
and read about statues according to goethean thought.

on my right, on my left, bucharest is and is not.

tr. Adam J. Sorkin and Mirela Surdulescu

STĂM OCHI ÎN OCHI

Mircea Cărtărescu

Stăm ochi în ochi, dar nu ştiu: ca doi amanţi
sau ca doi păianjeni? sau ca un om în oglindă? sau ca doi orbi
într-un azil? avem acelaşi drum.
Tu îmi reglezi oxitocina, vasopresina. Eu
ca o oglindă de telescop încerc să te prind
pe câţiva milimetri de viaţă. E ca şi cum
o larvă trichoforă ar încerca să-nţeleagă nu omul
ci viermele. Să spun că eşti un zeu? Că eşti totul? E o prostie.
Cel mai mic por al tău este totul. Şi totuşi
un ochi de aragaz sau clipa asta când bat la maşină
sunt mai măreţ e ca tine, căci ele *există*.

Mă imaginez cu privirea unei bacterii din propriul meu corp:
acolo,-n intestinul meu, papilele digestive
îi par quasari de neconceput. Dacă-ar înţelege una din ele
ar crede că *mă* înţelege.
Mă-nchipui mai amplu ca universul şi studiind un foton:
mi-aş închipui că te ştiu.

Aşa de naive religiile, mandalele, koanurile
căile spre iluminare şi lumina taborică
şi opus magnum; ciudată „viaţa de zi cu zi"
a budiştilor Zen. Rămâne din toate literatură frumoasă.
Swedenborg, Novalis... mescalina, stilul, eterul
mirosul de crin, stimulentele hormonale
sunt trucuri: totul e psihic, nimic nu-i *real*.

EYE TO EYE

by Mircea Cărtărescu

We're eye to eye, but I don't know: like two lovers
or like two spiders? like a man in a mirror? or like two blind faces
in an asylum? we're heading the same way.
You regulate my oxytocin, my vasopressin. I search
like a telescope mirror to capture you
on a few millimeters of life. It's as if
a trichophora larva were essaying to understand not man
but the worm. Shall I say that you're a god? That you're all there is?
                                    That's talking nonsense.
Your most minute pore is everything and more. And nonetheless
the eye of the gas burner or this instant when I'm clattering
                                    the typewriter keys
is greater than you, because they *exist*.

I imagine myself with the perspective of a bacterium inside my own body:
there, in my intestines, the digestive papillae
seem inconceivable quasars. If one of them possessed understanding
it would believe it understood *me*.
I fancy myself vaster than the universe and studying a photon:
I'd suppose I knew you.

So naive they are, then, the religions, mandalas, koans,
the paths to enlightenment and the Taboric light,
the magnum opus, the curious "life one day at a time"
of Zen Buddhists. What remains out of all these—beautiful literature.
Swedenborg, Novalis... mescaline, stylistics, ether
the perfume of the lily, hormonal stimulants
are simply tricks: everything is psychic, nothing *real*.

Tehnicile respiratorii
aplaudatul cu o singură palmă
abandonarea în fluxul vieţii, regăsirea unităţii lumii
stingerea, toate alegoriile, delirele, visele
sunt doar un şotron al minţii, jocuri pe calculator, fantomatică.
Astrologi ai creierului sunt mulţi.

9:20. Scriu în bucătărie. E o dimineaţă noroasă de mai.
Totul pare atât de real, de firesc: un deşteptător, o chiuvetă.
Dar floarea de cerceluş nu crede în existenţa mea.
Nici tu, care mă citeşti după ani şi ani.
De m-ai privi la video n-aş fi mai ireal pentru tine.
Totuşi exist, am puls, am un imaginar.

Eşti pe ambele părţi ale vieţii mele, ca o linie pe banda lui Möbius
eşti părinţii mei şi copilul lor, ca în butelia lui Klein
eşti ca un crab parazit, cu vinele băgate în vinele mele
cu faţa băgată în faţa mea, identic mie şi înglobat în mine,
eşti în fiecare obiect, căci fiecare obiect e o parte a mea,
uomo universale.
Stăm ochi în ochi, căci globii ochilor tăi
sunt în globii ochilor mei şi imaginea mea despre lume
e identică imaginii tale.

Dar aşa cum
o pagină scrisă e văzută identic
de înţelept şi de analfabet.

Techniques of breathing
one hand clapping
letting go into the flow of life, reexperiencing oneness with the world
extinction, all allegories, deliriums, dreams
are just a hopscotch of the mind, computer games, phantomatics.
Many are the astrologers of the brain.

9:20. I'm writing in the kitchen. It's a cloudy May morning.
All seems so real, natural: an alarm clock, a sink.
But the flowering lily-of-the-valley stalk doesn't believe in my existence.
Nor do you, you who are reading me after so many years.
If you saw me in a video I wouldn't seem unreal to you any longer.
All the same I exist, I have a pulse, I harbor my own imaginary.

You're on both sides of my life, like a line on a Möbius strip
you're my parents and their child, like in Klein's bottle
you're like a parasitic crab, with its veins thrust into my veins
its face thrust into my face, identical to me and integrated into me,
you're in each object, because each object is a part of me,
uomo universale.
We're eye to eye, because your eyeballs
are in my eyeballs, and my image of the world
is identical to your image.

But in exactly the way
a written page looks identical
to the learned and to the illiterate.

tr. Adam J. Sorkin and Radu Surdulescu

SCRISOAREA CU SUBȚIORI

Mircea Cărtărescu

tu ești scrisoarea cu subțiori
când mi te aduce, poștașul sună întotdeauna de două ori
te pun pe pat,
te scot din plicul tău de tergal înspicat
te netezesc, te citesc
de la hieroglifele genelor de tuș chinezesc
parcurg sfaturi adânci, sentințe profunde,
până ajung la două parafe rotunde
de roșie ceară
în cameră se lasă de seară
și totuși risc
să mai deslușesc câte ceva, până la asterisc
și până la semnătura-ncâlcită
de fire de antracită
indescifrabilă
dar foarte amabilă.
deși este beznă
mai descifrez P.S.-ul pe glezná
și după asta, în Braille
îți pipăi cu degetul alunițele bej și coraille
care spun o poveste bizară
cu o licornă și o fecioară.

nu te înțeleg cu totul și cred că nu te înțeleg deloc
scrisoarea ta face o burtică-ntr-un loc
și se sfârșește
oarecum în coadă de pește.

LETTER WITH ARMPITS

by Mircea Cărtărescu

you're a letter with armpits
when he delivers you, the post man always rings twice
I place you on the bed
I remove you from your envelope of striped polyester
I unfold you, I read you
from the hieroglyphics of your India-ink eyelashes
I scrutinize deep counsels, profound verdicts
until I arrive at two circular flourishes
of red sealing wax
evening settles in the room
nevertheless I still take the risk
of interpreting my findings, all the way to the asterisk
and the entangled signature
of anthracite fibers
indecipherable
but extremely eloquent.
although it's dark
I can still construe the P.S. on your ankle
and after that, with my finger,
I explicate the Braille of your beige and coral mole
which tells a bizarre legend
of a unicorn and a virgin.

I cannot understand you fully, I don't believe
                                        I understand you at all
your text gathers itself into a little mound in one place
and ends
somehow in a fishtail.

tu eşti o bancă de informaţii
numai curbe şi graţii
şi o consolă de calculator
numai claviatură şi dor.
tu rămâi scrisă într-o limbă de neconceput.

ce citesc? ce muşc? ce sărut?
o scrisoare de dragoste sau una financiară?
o foaie volantă incendiară?
un apel disperat? un blestem terific? o implorare-n
genunchi?
o telegramă care vesteşte o moarte năpraznică?
cine eşti tu? ce scrie pe pielea ta?

you're a data bank
with only curves and beguilements
a mainframe console
only keyboard and longing.
you stay written in an inconceivable language.

what am I reading? what am I biting?
                    what am I kissing?
a love letter or a financial prospectus?
an incendiary leaflet?
a desperate appeal? a terrifying curse?
                    a plea on bended knees?
a telegram which announces an unforeseen death?
who are you? what's spelled out on your skin?

tr. Adam J. Sorkin and Ioana Ieronim

VIAŢA MEA SE AGLOMEREAZĂ

Mircea Cărtărescu

câte imagini făceam când viaţa mea era goală!
era o deprivare senzorială, o nebunie ca a şahistului lui Zweig.
când scriam „Poemele de amor"
nimeni, nimeni nu era-n viaţa mea.
umblam de nebun pe Magheru fluierând Lennon
„sînt doar un tip gelos", dar nu eram gelos pe nimeni
căci nu exista nimeni: Jebe nu dădea telefoane
cu Traian mă certasem.
vroiam atât de mult să am o femeie a mea, o casă a mea
(seara intram la cinema „Volga" şi-mi dădeau lacrimile la orice tâmpen
i-am spus o dată lui Emil la „Cartea românească": „Ştii,
eu sufăr foarte mult de singurătate". A părut mirat
iar eu mă-ntrebam cum o fi să nu suferi de singurătate, din clasa
a zecea nu mi se mai întâmplase

de vreun an viaţa mea se aglomerează. totul e realist
şi tern ca o fotografie. am femeie.
am casă. am (dacă nu prieteni) amici.
citesc toate nopţile. alerg la slujbă cu 21.
dar nu sunt fericit şi sunt gelos pe cei singuri.

singurătatea mea — mă-ntâlnesc uneori cu tine
cum te-ntâlneşti pe stradă (lângă un lactobar) cu o veche prietenă
care a fost odată totul pentru tine
şi de care viaţa te-a despărţit.

MY LIFE'S GETTING CROWDED

by Mircea Cărtărescu

how many images I made when my life was empty!
It was a sensory deprivation, on obsession like that of Zweig's chess player.
while I was writing *The Poems of Love*
there was nobody, absolutely nobody in my life.
I would stroll like a mad man on Magheru Boulevard whistling Lennon's
"I'm just a jealous guy," but I was jealous of no one
or there was no one: Jebe didn't make phone calls
with Traian I'd had a falling out.
I wanted so much to have a woman of my own, a house of my own
(in the evening I went to the Volga cinema and shed tears over every dumb thing).
I once told Emil at The Romanian Book: "You know,
I really suffer from loneliness." He looked astounded,
and I wondered what it might be like not to suffer from loneliness; since tenth
grade that hadn't happened to me.

For about a year my life has been getting crowded. everything is realistic
and flat like a photograph. I have a woman.
I have a house. I have (if not friends) buddies.
every night I read. I rush to work on the 21 tram.
but I'm not happy and I'm jealous of the lonely.

my loneliness—I meet you sometimes
in the street (near a dairy bar) you might run into a former sweetheart
who once meant everything to you
and from whom life separated you.

ce pot să-ți spun? ai rămas la fel de frumoasă
dar mi-ești străină și nu te mai pot avea
și nu-ți mai pot lipi fața de-a mea decât prin geam, ca Delon și
                              Monica Vitti-n „Eclipsa"
acum ești singurătatea altuia
iar eu sunt un bărbat fără singurătate.

what's left to say to you? you remain just as beautiful
but now you're a stranger to me and I can't have you anymore
and I can no longer press my face to yours except through glass, like Delon
and Monica Vitti in L'Eclisse

now you're somebody else's loneliness
and I'm a man who's lost his loneliness.

tr. Adam J. Sorkin and Radu Surdulescu

Daniela Crăsnaru
Romania

AUSTERLOO

Daniela Crăsnaru

Şi detractorii şi fanii ştiu deopotrivă
unde-a pierdut şi unde a câştigat Generalul.
Chiar şi locuitorii din Sfânta Elena ştiu toţi
ce-a fost la Waterloo şi ce-a fost să fie Austerlitz.

Numai eu am încurcat totdeauna
înfrângerea cu victoria
câmpurile de bătălie, raportul de forţe
steagurile şi inamicul.
Şi asta n-a fost ca să fie tocmai o întâmplare
de elev corijent pus în solda
frivolei posterităţi. Toată victoria mea
a fost mai degrabă înfrângere.
Toată prada luată de armata mea de cuvinte
mărşăluind buimacă
prin această eternă siberie a îndoielii
s-a dovedit a fi îngrăşată cu sângele meu.
Chiar şi „mirosul morţii atât de aproape de
                                    mirosul dragostei
ca violetul de indigo în discul luminii".

Cu cele mai bune divizii pe jumătate
anii mei îmbuibând humusul acestor coli de hârtie.
Cu trăgătorii mei de elită
striviţi între coperţile unor cărţi.

Austerloo, 14 iunie
şi mâna mea scriind jurnalul de front fără să ştie
dacă e moartă
sau vie.

AUSTERLOO

by Daniela Crăsnaru

Both his critics and his fans well know
where the General lost and where he carried the day.
Every resident of Saint Helena knows, too,
what was at Austerlitz and what had to be at Waterloo.

Only I, I always confused
the defeat with the victory,
the battlefields, the balance of forces,
the pennants and the enemy.
And this isn't the simple case
of a student who was left back and made a mercenary
for frivolous posterity. All my victories
turn out defeats.
All the plunder captured by my army of words
marching disoriented
through an endless Siberia of doubt
has proved to be fed to bursting with my own blood.
Even "the odor of death as close to the odor of love
as violet to indigo in light's spectrum."

With my crack divisions cut down by half,
my years gorging the humus of this sheet of paper.
With my sharpshooters
crushed between the covers of my books.

My hand writing this battlefield log without a clue
as to whether it's alive
or dead.
June 14, Austerloo.

tr. Adam J. Sorkin with the poet

INCENDIUL

Daniela Crăsnaru

Brusc
ar trebui să aprind reflectorul
să caut lupa
cea mai puternică
să umblu prin măruntaiele
piramidei de vorbe.
Cu sânge rece să spintec
acest fabulos animal
care nu mai vrea
să mă-nghită odată.
Să dau foc
peliculei voalate
in care continui să văd
ceea ce nu e şi nu e
şi nu e.
Şi chiar acum să renunţ
la cohorta de palide perifraze
şi sinonime
ale singurătăţii.

THE FIRE

by Daniela Crăsnaru

All of a sudden
I must switch on the searchlights
hunt for
the most powerful magnifying glass
crawl through the viscera
of this pyramid of words.
Slaughter in cold blood
this fabled animal
which no longer wants
to swallow me.
Set fire
to this exposed film
on which I continue to see
what is not and what is not
and what is not.
And in this same instant
renounce cohorts of pale periphrases
and synonyms
for solitude.

tr. Adam J. Sorkin with the poet

INDIGO, VIOLET

Daniela Crăsnaru

În burta calului
grecii beau vin şi se pregătesc
de victorie.
Înaintea ultimei zile
troienii nu ştiu
că mâine e ultima zi.
Războiul de treizeci de ani
e şi el în cel de-al treizecilea an
în penultima zi
a celui de-al treizecilea an
şi soldaţii lui nu ştiu
că mâine e ultima zi.
Războiul de o sută de ani
e în cel de-al nouăzeci şi nouălea an
în ultima zi
a celui de-al nouăzeci şi nouălea an
şi nici soldaţii lui
nu ştiu că azi e ultima zi
deşi
mirosul morţii se simte
de la o mie de leghe
mirosul morţii
atât de apropiat de mirosul dragostei
ca violetul de indigo
în discul luminii.

INDIGO, VIOLET

by Daniela Crăsnaru

In the horse's belly
the Greeks guzzle wine and get set
for victory.
Before the final day
the Trojans have no idea
tomorrow is the final day.
The Thirty Years' War, too,
is in the thirtieth year.
On the penultimate day
of its thirtieth year
the soldiers likewise have no idea
tomorrow is the final day.
The Hundred Years' War
is in the ninety-ninth year.
On the final day
of its ninety-ninth year
not one of the soldiers
has any idea today is the final day
although
the odor of death is discernible
from a thousand leagues off,
the odor of death
as close to the odor of love
as violet to indigo
in light's spectrum.

În dreptul inimii tale
un cadran de piatră
un minutar
care foarte curând
şi el va-mpietri.

Indigo, violet
mirosul dragostei şi al morţii
doi fluturi gemeni
într-o crisalidă de lut.

În dreptul inimii tale
un cadran de piatră un minutar
împietrit.

Astăzi nu, astăzi nu, poate *mâine*—
cuvânt şerpuind într-un spasm ultim
la colţul gurii-ncleştate.
Mâine.
Vopseaua purpurie, firul de sânge
sub masca perfectă a faraonului.

Before your heart
a sundial of stone,
a minute hand
that all too soon
will turn to stone.

Indigo, violet:
the odor of love and the odor of death,
a pair of butterflies
twinned in a clay chrysalis.

Before your heart
a sundial of stone, a minute hand
stone still.

Not today, not today, maybe *tomorrow*,
the word contorted in a final spasm
snaking from the corner of clenched lips.
Tomorrow.
Dye of purple, thin dribble of blood
beneath the perfect mask of the Pharaoh.

tr. Adam J. Sorkin

MICILE DESCOPERIRI GEOGRAFICE

Daniela Crăsnaru

Ce pământ fericit
aş fi putut fi
ce pământ fericit am mai fost
ce americă sub călcâiele
lui columb—între nouă şi zece
seara între orele nouă şi zece
lecţia noastră de geografie
golf cu golf, vale cu vale
cu mâinile lui desenate
pe harta asta amară.
Ah micile
şi marile canioane ale singurătăţii
strivite de hohotul
a o mie de niagare.
Între nouă şi zece lecţia
de geografie până când
veni el, micul demon din nord
din extremul nord
de la gheţuri
micul demon al lucidităţii
cu lămpaşul în stânga
cu dreapta lui limpede
rece precum cristalul
mă smulse de-acolo şi mă dădu
cu capul de pragul de sus:
Care columb, ce columb
ăsta dimineaţa între şapte şi nouă
se dă vasco da gama

LESSER GEOGRAPHICAL DISCOVERIES

by Daniela Crăsnaru

What a happy land
I could have been
what a happy land I used to be
what an America under Columbus's
heels—between nine and ten
between nine and ten in the evening
our geography lesson
gulf by gulf valley by valley
with his hands drawn
on this bitter map.
Oh the lesser
and the grand canyons of loneliness
overwhelmed by the cascading laughter
of a thousand Niagaras.
Between nine and ten
the geography lesson until he
showed up, the little demon from the north
from the far north
from the glaciers
the little demon of lucidity
a lantern in his left hand
who with his translucent right hand
cold like crystal
uprooted me and threw me out
cracking my head against the lintel:
Which Columbus, what Columbus
this one between seven and nine in the morning
pretends to be Vasco da Gama

şi descoperă india
profesionist al iluziei e
şarlatan, profesor cu ora
mai zise scârbit micul demon
refugiindu-se-n nord
în extremul nord sub calota
de gheaţă
în timp ce mâinile lui
ale conchistadorului
se umplură deodată de toate
mirodeniile indiilor de dimineaţă
şi niagara căzu
ca o cortină de plumb
peste lecţia noastră de geografie
peste pământul fericit umilit
care aş fi putut fi, care
am fost, care sunt
astăzi şi mâine şi mâine
şi mâine.

and discovers India
he is a professional of illusion
a charlatan, a mere temporary part-time instructor
sneered the little demon in disgust
taking refuge in his north
in the far north under the polar
ice cap
while his hands
a conquistador's
filled suddenly with all
the spices of an Indies morning
and Niagara plummeted
like a lead curtain
over our geography lesson
over the happy humiliated land
which I could have been, which
I was, which I am
today and tomorrow and tomorrow
and tomorrow.

tr. Adam J. Sorkin with the poet

MEZZO DEL CAMIN

Daniela Crăsnaru

O să treacă toate, o să treacă şi viaţa
şi zmeul zmeilor n-a mai venit
iar eu am obosit să-mi tot inventez peisajul
                şi întâmplările
iubirile şi decepţiile, revolta şi laşitatea
şi toate celelalte teme din lucrarea de diplomă
a filologului premiant.
Eu
care locuiesc în somptuoasa singurătate a ficţiunii
plângând cu ajutorul cuvântului lacrimă şi iubind
cu ajutorul altui cuvânt, în fine
eu
care am ajuns un simplu pronume in propriul meu text
atât de urât
îmi e mie cu mine, cu mine, cu mine,
şi-atât mi-e de dor
de un monstru tăcut, de-o fiară tristă,
de-o fiinţă vie
de altundeva decât de la mine
din Poezie.

MEZZO DEL CAMIN

by Daniela Crăsnaru

All things will pass, even this life,
and no wonderful wise wizard has ever appeared.
I am grown tired of always inventing the landscapes and events,
the loves and deceits, the rebellion and cowardice,
and the rest of the main themes in the diploma paper
of the top graduate in philology.
I
who live in the sumptuous solitude of fiction,
crying with the help of the word *tear* and loving
with the help of another word,
I
who became a simple pronoun in my own text,
so sick of myself and frightened for me, for me, for me,
in the end, I yearn
for a silent monster, a sad wordless entity,
a living, breathing creature to be set free
from somewhere else than my very own
Poetry.

tr. Adam J. Sorkin with the poet

RĂSCRUCE

Ileana Mălăncioiu

Între poezia care face ordine
Şi cea care face dezordine
O cale pentru cel înfricoşat
O fiinţă care coboară din paradis.

Mi-am deschis creierul ca niciodată
Cu propriile mele unghii
Şi tu ieşi din el *pururi tînăr*
Înfăşurat în manta-ţi.

Acolo unde îţi stă trupul
Îţi va sta şi sufletul strig
Şi spaţiul se umple de strigăt
Ca de păsări de pradă.

Un plisc imens coboară încet
Scormoneşte în carnea ta crudă
Şi îţi trage încet de pe oase
Materia mea cenuşie.

CROSSROADS

by Ileana Mălăncioiu

Between poetry that creates order
and the one which creates disorder
there is a way for the fearful ones:
a being who descends from paradise.

I have opened my brain as never
before, with my own nails—
and you emerge—*eternally young
and enveloped in your mantle.*

Where your body now stands,
your soul shall be rooted—I shout,
and the space fills with my shout
as with birds of prey.

An immense beak slowly descends
to scavenge your living flesh—
yes, it slowly tears off your bones
my mind's grey matter.

> *tr. Ellen Hinsey and*
> *Anca Cristofovici*

NU POT SĂ MĂ PLÎNG

Ileana Mălăncioiu

Nu pot să mă plîng de foame,
Hrana mea din ceruri vine,
Dar mi-e teamă pentru zeul
Ce se va hrăni cu mine.

Sînt prea neagră, sînt prea tristă,
Jertfa mea poate să-i pară
Şi mai slabă decît este
Şi mai rea şi mai amară.

Sîngele-ar putea să-l verse
Într-un cîmp frumos cu maci,
Carnea ar putea rămîne
Să se-mpartă la săraci.

I HAVE NO COMPLAINTS

by *Ileana Mălăncioiu*

About hunger I have no complaints,
all my food comes from the sky—
but I fear for the unlucky god
who chooses me for his sustenance.

I am too dark, I am too sad,
my offering might seem to him
even more meagre than it is—
even more stale, even more bitter.

Still he could spill my blood
over a fine field of poppies,
and my flesh would remain
to be doled out to the poor.

tr. Ellen Hinsey and
Anca Cristofovici

ÎMI IAU ÎN PALME CAPUL

Ileana Mălăncioiu

Îmi iau în palme capul golit încet de visuri
Cade ca o minge elastică
Pe pămîntul neted ca-n palmă
Din grădina fantastică.

Se poate spune că a fost rotund,
Se poate spune că a fost atins
Cum trebuie de mîna ageră
A celui neînvins.

Mai mult nu se poate spune,
Ce mai interesează acum că era tuns
Ca să se rostogolească mai bine,
Sau că era de nepătruns.

E linişte şi vine jucătorul
Cu pieptul plin de visele ucise
Şi le suflă-napoi în capul rostogolit
Prin pleoapele proaspăt închise.

MY HEAD IN MY HANDS

by Ileana Mălăncioiu

My head in my hands, drained of dreams
falls like a rubber ball
on the ground—that even palm
of the fantastic garden.

It can be said that it was round,
it can be said that it was touched
in grace by the agile hand
of the undefeated.

No more can be said.
What matters now is that it was cropped
to roll better—
and that it was impenetrable.

Silence. A player comes,
his own breast full of severed dreams.
And through the eyelids, freshly shut,
he breathes a dream into the runaway head.

*tr. Ellen Hinsey and
Anca Cristofovici*

DARUL

Marin Sorescu

— Îţi voi dovedi că toate tablourile sunt false,
Spuse specialistul, scoţându-şi lupa
Pe care tocmai o primise cadou
Din planeta Marte.

Colecţionarul zâmbi, îl amuza ideea,
Pânzele lui deveniseră etalon
Pentru identificarea maeştrilor din toată lumea,
Cheltuise pe ele averea câtorva generaţii
Înainte şi înapoi.

— Să începem de la dreapta spre stânga,
Priveşte acest Tizian!
Într-adevăr, în lupă se vede stângăcia execuţiei,
Tabloul fusese pictat de un elev fără talent,
Într-o oră de desen.

— În fundul sufletului mă rodea un fel de îndoială
În privinţa lui, şopti galben colecţionarul.
Dar acel Rafael, pe care-l studiezi acum,
Dacă e o copie,
Însăşi mâna lui Dumnezeu a făcut-o, ha, ha, ha!

— Priveşte, şi cercetătorul care n-avea chef de glumă
Îi arătă numărul de serie înregistrat
În pupilele madonei.
Pe la mijlocul sălii nici n-apuca să îndrepte
Lupa spre ele

THE GIFT

by Marin Sorescu

"I'm going to prove that all your paintings are fakes,"
The art expert said, taking out the magnifying glass
He'd just received as a present
From the planet Mars.

The collector saw amusement in the idea and smiled.
His canvases had become the standard
For identification of the masters from everywhere in the world.
He'd lavished on them the fortune of several generations
Gone by and yet to come.

"Let's start from right to left.
Look at this Titian!"
Indeed, through the glass, its clumsy execution could be seen.
"This canvas has been painted by an untalented beginner
In a drawing class."

"In the depths of my soul I had some doubts
On that score," whispered the pale collector.
"But that Raphael, the one you're examining now,
If it's a copy,
God's hand itself made it, ha, ha, ha!"

"Take a look!" And the expert, who had no taste for humor,
Showed him the registered serial number
Stamped on the Madonna's pupil.
By the time the expert reached the middle of the gallery, he'd hardly point
His magnifying glass at them

Şi tablourile cădeau singure.
În faţa ultimei pânze, Rembrandt milionarul!—colecţionarul
Îşi duse mâna la inimă şi căzând
Din gura lui zburară lilieci.

Specialistul colindă apoi prin multe muzee
Pe care le umplu de ridicol.

Nici măcar ramele nu erau veritabile,
Lupa neînduplecată scotea la iveală
Lucruri groaznice.

Toţi marii maeştri fuseseră ucişi
După primele trăsături de penel,
Şi ucigaşii le furaseră numele,
Pictaseră în continuare cu uleiurile lor,
Moarte şi ele,
O dată cu sângele cel adevărat.

Aşa se golirá galeriile,
Achizitorii nepricepuţi înfundară puşcăriile.

În urma omului cu lupa se întindea un pustiu de moarte
Şi el era tot mai trist.

Odată îi veni în gând
Să îndrepte lupa spre strada pe care mergea
Şi observă cu uimire că era falsă,
Strada adevărată se afla mult mai încolo.

And the paintings would fall on their own.
In front of the last canvas, Rembrandt the millionaire!—the collector
Raised his hand to his heart and, as he crumpled,
Bats fluttered from his mouth.

The art expert then strolled through many a museum,
All of which he filled with derision.

Not even the frames were authentic.
The inexorable glass brought to view
Dreadful things.

All the great masters had been murdered
After the first strokes of their brush,
And the murderers had stolen their names,
Continuing to paint with their oils,
Which had died, too,
At the same time as their real blood.

This is how the galleries became emptied.
The unwitting benefactors were whisked off to prison.

Behind the man with the magnifying glass extended a wasteland of death,
And he became sadder and sadder.

Suddenly, he had the inspiration
To direct the lens at the street he was walking in,
And he noticed, with astonishment, that it too was fake.
The real street was much farther away.

Privi oraşul — era fals, copacii falşi,
Şi începu să plângă.

Plângând cu hohote şi tremurând tot,
În afara mâini care ţinea teribilul instrument
El o porni foarte bătrân înainte,
Continuând să desfiinţeze lumea.

He looked at the town—it was a fake, the trees were fakes.
And he began to cry.

Sobbing, trembling in every limb,
Except the hand which held the terrible instrument,
He started off again, now very old,
Continuing to abolish the world.

tr. Adam J. Sorkin and
Lidia Vianu

EXPANSIUNEA UNIVERSULUI

Marin Sorescu

— Petre, zice Dumnezeu,
Ţie nu ţi se întâmplă să faci de două ori
Acelaşi lucru?
Uite, eu am creat lumea
De vreo câteva ori,
Pentru că am uitat c-am creat-o.
Parcă aveam de gând să fac azi ceva
Extraordinar, îmi zic,
Ce să fac? Ce să fac?
Şi mai trântesc o lume —
Iarăşi şi iarăşi.

— Am auzit eu ceva de lumi paralele,
De fuga spre roşu, sau cam aşa ceva,
Zice Petru,
Dar nu credeam că intenţionat.
— Ce intenţionat, eşti copil? E tot aia,
Făcută de mai multe ori, fiindcă uit.

Să-mi dai ceva de memorie.

THE EXPANSION OF THE UNIVERSE

by Marin Sorescu

"Peter," says God,
"Does it ever happen to you that you do the very same thing
More than once?
For instance, I've created the world
A few times over,
Because I forgot I'd already created it.
It seems I get a notion to make something
Extraordinary, but then...
What was it? What was it?
And so I slap down another world —
Not once but again and again."

"I've heard something about parallel worlds,
About the red shift and the such,"
Says Peter,
"But I'd no idea this were on purpose."
"On purpose? Don't be a ninny. They're all the selfsame one
Made many times over, because I keep forgetting.

You know, Peter, can you give me anything for the memory?"

tr. Adam J. Sorkin and
Gabriela Dragnea

CĂCIULA

Marin Sorescu

Ce e moartea altceva
Decât o misterioasă dispariție a lucrurilor?

Îi dispare întâi căciula.
Era pe cap, a pus-o pe scaun
Și nu mai e pe scaun.
Caută bine — și nu mai e nici scaunul!
O fi pus-o pe pat? Dar unde e patul?
Pe clanța ușii? (Excelent cuier uneori).
Nici tu clanță, nici tu ușă. S-au pierdut în hău.
Și așa crește golul din jur...

Și asta se repetă zi cu zi...
Totuși, fără o continuitate strictă,
Căci uneori căciula apare. Reapare.
Se pomenește cu ea pe cap.

Se așează pe scaun. Deschide ușa,
Pune mâna pe clanță.
Lucrurile stau cuminți la locul lor.
Se lasă pipăite. Se gâdilă și îl gâdilă la
Buricele degetelor. Chicotesc. Chicotește.
Acest vino-ncoace al materiei. Sarea vieții!
Până când... speriat:
— Nevastă, căciula!

THE FUR HAT

by Marin Sorescu

What is death
But a mysterious disappearance of things?

First it's his fur hat that disappears.
It was on his head, he put it on the chair,
And it's no longer there.
He keeps searching — there's no chair, either!
Could he have put it on the bed? But where's the bed?
Hung it from the door handle? (Sometimes a most excellent peg.)
Neither a handle nor a door. Lost in the abyss.
That's how the void grows all around, all around...

This repeats itself day after day...
However, in no regular progression,
For sometimes the hat simply appears. Reappears.
He finds himself with the fur hat on his head.

He sits down in the chair. Opens the door,
Rests his hand on the handle.
Things obediently assume their place.
They let themselves be touched. They tickle and tickle
Each other's fingertips. He giggles. They giggle.
Oh, the sly come-hither of matter. The salt of life!
Until he... suddenly terrified:
"Woman, my hat!"

Sau: Nu ştii unde am pus ochelarii?
— Iar începi?
— Nu încep, continui.

Repet: Ce e moartea altceva
Decât o misterioasă dispariţie a lucrurilor?

Or: "Do you know where I put my glasses?"
"You're starting at it again!"
"I don't start anything, I just keep at it."

I rest my case: What is death
But a mysterious disappearance of things?

tr. Adam J. Sorkin and
Gabriela Dragnea

EU ŞI CELĂLALT

Marin Sorescu

Merg repede, repede
Nu ştiu ce-mi dă prin gând, mă opresc,
Mă întorc şi mă izbeşte, venind din urmă,
Haloul meu, principiul activ,
Fiinţa mea astrală, grăuntele de adevăr,
În fine, aşa-zisa mea personalitate.

Ca duhoarea fiarei,
Cea care trădează vânatul,
Adulmecat de câini.
— Miroase a om, zic.
Te-am prins. Unde te duci?

— Nicăieri.
Mă ţin şi eu după tine,
Pe potecă.

I AND THE OTHER

by Marin Sorescu

I'm walking in a great hurry
I don't know what suddenly crosses my mind, so I stop quickly,
I turn around, and from right behind me,
My aura slams into me, my vital principle,
My astral being, the grain of truth,
In short, my personality — so-called.

Like the smell of the beast,
Which betrays the game,
Sniffed by the hounds.
"It stinks of man," I cry out.
"I've caught you now. Where do you think you're headed?"

"Nowhere.
I'm just trailing behind you,
Along the path."

tr. Adam J. Sorkin and
Gabriela Dragnea

TABLOURI

Marin Sorescu

Toate muzeele se tem de mine,
Fiindcă de câte ori stau o zi-ntreagă
În faţa unui tablou,
A doua zi se anunţă
Dispariţia tabloului.

În fiecare noapte sunt prins furând
Într-o altă parte a lumii,
Dar mie nici nu-mi pasă
De gloanţele ce-mi şuieră pe la ureche,
Şi de câinii lup care-mi cunosc acum
Mirosul urmelor
Mai bine decât îndrăgostiţii
Parfumul iubitei.

Vorbesc tare cu pânzele ce-mi primejduiesc viaţa,
Le-agăţ de nori şi de copaci
Şi mă dau înapoi să am perspectivă.
Cu maeştrii „italieni" poţi să legi uşor o conversaţie.
Ce gălăgie de culori!
Şi din cauza asta
Cu ei sunt foarte repede prins,
Văzut şi auzit de la distanţă,
Parcă aş duce-n braţe papagali.

Cel mai greu se fură Rembrandt:
Întinzi mâna şi dai de-ntuneric —
Te-apucă groaza, oamenii lui nu au trupuri,
Ci numai ochii închişi în beciuri întunecoase.

PAINTINGS

by Marin Sorescu

All the museums are afraid of me,
Because whenever I spend an entire day
In front of a painting,
The next day they announce
Its disappearance.

Every night I'm caught stealing
In another distant corner of the world.
But I don't give a damn about
The bullets whizzing past my ears,
Or the bloodhounds which now know
The scent of my footprints
Better than lovers know
Their beloved's favorite perfume.

I talk to the canvases that imperil my life.
I hang them from clouds and trees
And stand back to view them in perspective.
You can easily strike up a conversation with the Italian masters.
What a clamor of colors!
And for this reason
I'm caught with them almost at once,
Espied and overheard from far, far away,
As if I had parrots perched on my arms.

The hardest to steal is Rembrandt:
You reach out your hand and touch darkness—
Dread clutches you, his figures have no bodies,
Just eyes shut over dark cellars.

Pânzele lui Van Gogh sunt nebune,
Se-nvârtesc şi se dau peste cap,
Şi trebuie să ţii bine de ele
Cu amândouă mâinile,
Că sunt supte de-o forţă din lună.

Nu ştiu de ce Breugel mă face să plâng,
El nu era mai bătrân decât mine,
Dar i s-a spus bătrânul,
Fiindcă pe toate le ştia când a murit.

Şi eu caut să-nvăţ de la el,
Dar nu pot să-mi ţin lacrimile,
Care-mi curg pe ramele lui de aur
Când fug cu anotimpurile la subsuoară.

Cum vă spuneam, în fiecare noapte
Fur câte un tablou
Cu o dexteritate de invidiat.
Drumul fiind însă foarte lung,

Sunt prins până la urmă
Şi ajung acasă noaptea târziu,
Obosit şi sfâşiat de câini,
Ţinând în mână o reproducere ieftină.

Van Gogh's canvases have gone crazy.
They whirl and turn head over heels,
You've got to hold fast
With both hands,
As they're sucked in by a force on the moon.

I don't know why Breughel makes me weep.
He wasn't any older than I am,
But they called him the elder,
Because when he died he knew all there is to know.

I strive to learn from him, too,
But I can't restrain my tears,
Which stream along the gilded frames
While I flee with his seasons under my arm.

So, as I was explaining, every night
I manage to steal some painting or other
With an enviable dexterity.
But since it's so long a way,

I always get caught in the end
And reach home late at night,
Torn by the dogs and weary,
Grasping in my hands a cheap reproduction.

tr. Adam J. Sorkin and
Lidia Vianu

НЕ УДЕЛЯЙ МНЕ МНОГО ВРЕМЕНИ

Bella Akhmadulina

Не уделяй мне много времени,
вопросов мне не задавай.
Глазами добрыми и верными
руки моей не задевай.

Не проходи весной по лужицам,
по следу следа моего.
Я знаю — снова не получится
из этой встречи ничего.

Ты думаешь, что я из гордости
хожу, с тобою не дружу?
Я не из гордости — из горести
так прямо голову держу.

DON'T WASTE YOUR TIME

by Bella Akhmadulina

Don't waste your time and mine
with flattering "whens" and "whys".
Don't caress my hands with your
faithful-doggy eyes.

There's no point following me
through spring puddles, soggy air.
Even if we meet by chance
it won't lead anywhere.

Because my head's held high
you think we're kept apart
by pride. Don't blame my pride;
it is my heavy heart.

tr. Diana Der-Hovanessian
with Professor David Sloane

ДРУГОЕ

Bella Akhmadulina

Что сделалось? Зачем я не могу,
уж целый год не знаю, не умею
слагать стихи и только немоту
тяжелую в моих губах имею?

Вы скажете — но вот уже строфа,
четыре строчки в ней, она готова.
Я не о том. Во мне уже стара
привычка ставить слово после слова.

Прядок этот ведает рука.
Я не о том. Как это прежде было?
Когда происходило — не строка —
другое что-то. Только что? — Забыла.

Да, то, другое, разве знало страх,
когда шалило голосом так смело,
само, как смех, смеялось на устах
и плакало, как плач, если хотело?

SOMETHING ELSE

by Bella Akhmadulina

I don't know why I can't make
verses anymore. Writer's block?
Now for almost a year
the flow of poems has stopped.

But, you say, what is this stanza then
with four sides like a wall?
Yes, but it came from habit
placing word after word, that's all.

My hand proceeds to scrawl.
But process is not the point.
Formerly something else was involved,
something that is lost.

Whatever was frightened away
used to arrive like tears
or laughter unbid, and surprised
to find itself here.

tr. Diana Der-Hovanessian
with Professor David Sloane

ЦАРСКИЕ ЖЕНЫ

Valentina Borovitskaya

Древний мир был наивен.
По царским могилам
Обнаружили мы,
Что их жен хоронили
В тот же час,
Облачив погребальною тканью,
Чтобы смерть их была, как второе венчанье.

Наконец, неразлучны.
А сколько тревоги
Было ей в ожиданьях
На белой дороге,
Сколько было прощаний
Трагично-безмолвных.
Из особого воска
Все царские жены.

Что им делать,
Оставшись в реальном и сущем.
Думать все о былом
Да о хлебе насущном.
Наблюдать,
Как, тщеславья скрывать не умея,
Делят царских коней
Подлецы и плебеи.

В древнем мире забытом,
Наивном и мудром,
Умереть вместе с ним
Было делом нетрудным.
Эта пара одна-неделима
На свете.
И другого такого
Ей больше не встретить.

EMPERORS' WIVES

by Valentina Borovitskaya

The ancient world was naive.
We discovered
In the graves of emperors
That they were buried
With their wives,
Who were dressed in funeral fabrics
So their death was like a second marriage.

Finally, inseparable.
But how much anxiety
For her, all that waiting
On the white road.
How many farewells
Tragically silent.
Such special people
Are all emperors' wives.

What could they do,
Remaining in the real and the present.
To think all the time about the past
And of the daily bread.
To observe,
How the scoundrels and plebeians,
Not knowing how to hide conceit,
Share emperor's horses among them.

In the ancient world, forgotten
Naive and wise,
To die together with him
Was not a difficult task.
That's one unique couple
In the world.
And another one like him
She is unlikely to find.

tr. Dasha Čulić Nisula

ДВОРЦОВАЯ НАБЕРЕЖНАЯ

Valentina Borovitskaya

Когда над белою Невой
Плывет мерцанье белой ночи,
И жизнь ушедшая не хочет
Исчезнуть в дымке голубой,
Тогда, как чернь на серебре,
Проступит кружево балконов,
И белоснежные колонны
Расскажут повесть о поре
Таких интриг, таких свершений,
Когда царили над страной
То гений зла, то мудрый гений.
На миг, на несколько минут
Дворцы прервут свое молчанье,
Заговорят — и оживут
Их времена, дела и тайны.

PALACE EMBANKMENT

by Valentina Borovitskaya

When above the white Neva
Sails a glimmer of the White Night,
And life past does not want to
Disappear in the pale blue haze,
Then, like niello on silver,
Laced balconies appear
And snow white columns
Tell a story of a time
Of such intrigues, of such things done,
When over the land ruled
A wise genius or a genius of evil.
For a moment, for several minutes
The palaces break their silence,
And begin to speak—and their times,
Deeds and secrets become alive.

tr. Dasha Čulić Nisula

В ЭТОМ ТИХОМ И СВЕТЛОМ КРАЮ

Tamara Kazakova

В этом тихом и светлом краю,
Где беседует мирно со мной
Золотистая тварь, стрекоза,
На мятежную душу мою
На мгновенье нисходит покой,
Словно вечность мне глянет в глаза.

Только здесь ощущаю, как я
Стала почкой, пчелой, муравьем,
Лепестком голубого цветка.
Здесь на тайным приют бытия
Проливаются теплым дождем
Быстротающие облака.

Но уже в отлаленье гремит
За горой притаившийся гром.
Чертят что-то на кульманах дня
Молнии. Накренился зенит —
И тайфун сотрясает мой дом,
Изгоняя из рая меня.

IN THIS QUIET AND LIGHT LAND

by Tamara Kazakova

In this quiet and light land,
Where the golden creature, the dragonfly,
Talks with me peacefully,
Calm descends for a moment
Upon my rebellious soul,
As if eternity looks me in the eye.

Only here I feel like a
Bud, a bee, or an ant,
A petal of a pale blue flower.
Here, in the secret shelter of being
Warm rain is pouring
Under the cover of melting clouds.

But already, in the distance, thunder
Hides behind the mountain.
The lightning is drawing something on the drafting
table of the day. The zenith tilts —
A typhoon shakes my home,
And throws me out of paradise.

tr. Dasha Čulić Nisula
with the poet

241

"ДУШИ ПОГРУЖЕНЫ В МОЛЧАНЬЕ"
(M. Maeterlinck)

Tamara Kazakova

В молчании есть логика своя:
Так значимы несказанные речи,
Что их услышав, причащаюсь я
Сладчайшего из всех земных наречий.

Безжалостно стремление назвать,
Принять за суть обманчивость покрова,
Но вот на нас нисходит благодать —
И тишина нам заменяет слово.

Помилуй, господи, всех малых сих,
Витийствующих, шепчущих, кричащих,
Прими как жертву мой негромкий стих
И сопричисли К Ордену Молчащих.

"SOULS ARE IMMERSED IN SILENCE"
(M. Maeterlinck)

by Tamara Kazakova

There is certain logic in silence:
So significant are unuttered words,
That on hearing them, I take a sacrament
Of the sweetest earthly tongue.

To name things is a dangerous desire
To take this deceit for essence,
But here grace descends upon us
And silence replaces the word.

Have mercy, Lord, on all the little ones,
The meek, the loud, and the eloquent,
Accept my humble verse as a sacrifice
And admit me into the Order of the Silent.

tr. Dasha Čulić Nisula
with the poet

LULLABIES TO FEAR

by Saša Vegri

I.

Like bread and fruit
they take my wishes
and leave them carefree anywhere.
They scatter my time
to all corners of the garden
and summon me inconsolably
when a snail slides on a trail
or some fallen leaf
resembles a punt.
I hide in front of them
behind so-called apathy
or simply
behind the doorway
so they don't disperse everything
I want to keep for myself.
But they follow me
from the fence of my glance
and there they camp
under the autumn sky
and my eyes:
small, brave,
inquisitive.
In an instant
curious
they come out to the edge of the sidewalk
and run after a dog
or a car,
as if they run into my arms.
And I run after them
confused and frightened,
I run, but I never catch up with them.

II.

And they run.
They tied the umbilical cord
of my worries
and laugh
in a yellow voice,
big, big children
of my embrace.
Yet, when I sew their clothes
and weave butterflies and dolls
in colorful threads,
they look back anxiously at my work
and continually measure
the stitched treasure.
If they lose my needle,
they lose it
as if no one will
ever find it again.
And they run,
continuously run
from somewhere to somewhere.
If I have to cross their tracks
spread across the entire floor —
and which I don't see well —
I step on them;
they scold me
and are angry.
They call me an elephant
until I become one
who carries them across a desert.
While they shout on my back
and pull me by the hair,
the tracks are
long gone.

They continuously ask
I play with them.
Then they leave me
like they leave a lid
or little rags.
And I straighten out
the toys
and myself,
I put myself in the right place.
And my right place is
now here
now there,
continuously somewhere
on the trail of their games.

tr. Dasha Čulić Nisula

TO A BIRD IN A CAGE A CHILD IN A CAGE

by Ifigenija Zagoričnik

it's easy to pull a child's hair
poke out its eyes
blow it up
rape
rear
you can stop it
you can hold it by the ankles two meters high
you can throw it on the floor against the wall
you can drop it from the twentieth floor
you can hold it hanging by the wrists
throw it out of a window onto the balcony or a train
you can dump its head in dung
dress it to your taste
you can love it
smother it with embrace
you can poison it
infect it with a kiss
you cannot take it seriously
you can leave it in the lurch
to wait
to hope
leave it in the hot sun
to thirst

you can forbid a child
convince it request
order promise
give give not give
you can let it down a street

to a child you can explain everything
to a fly break its wings
to a chicken chop its head
to a cat drown its litter

tr. Dasha Čulić Nisula

UNDER THE SAME ROOF

by Ifigenija Zagoričnik

let's stay
each on our own side

each in our own bed
sleeps
each with our own blanket
covered
each on our own side of the table
lives
each our own way

each from the other side of the street
we meet
each in a different district
lives
each in another city
each in another country
each in another hemisphere
each in another world
we meet

each in our own world
staring
under the same roof
let's remain
squeezed
one to another something other
one to another each moment
different

each moment as if it were the first
each moment as if it were the last

different from what we are toward others
let's remain to one another

tr. Dasha Čulić Nisula

НІЧНІ ЛІТАКИ

Natalka Bilotserkivets

Нічні літаки пролітають незримо,
Сніги опадають на вулиці міста,
О першій згасають бліді ліхтарі,
Зникають останні трамваі...

                     Тепер
Лишаються тільки будинки поснулі,
Дерева геть темні,
             та серце гаряче —
Як грудочка тепла живої землі.

Ці дні, наче роки,
                 минають поволі,
Ці дні невиразних туманів, снігів,
Сніданків, обідів, подій монотонних...
Але прислухайся —
            колись уночі
Повернуться в брамі трагічні ключі,
І видива спогадів,
               нам незнайомих,
Постануть крізь гуркіт нічних літаків.

Освітиться в серці розбите вікно
Далекої школи — чи, може, собору,
Чи, може, майдани розхитаних вулиць,
Чи, може, галявини зимних лісів...
І хори ослаблих ламких голосів
Співатимуть з неба старі колискові
І перші слова неживих букварів.

NIGHT PLANES

by Natalka Bilotserkivets

Night planes fly past invisibly,
Snow falls on the city street,
At one AM they turn off the dim street lamps,
And the last tram cars disappear...

                Only
drowsy buildings are left,
Trees are dark,
             but the heart is hot
Like a warm clod of living earth.

These days like years
             pass slowly,
These days of ill-defined fog, of snows,
Breakfasts, lunches, and monotonous events...
But listen—
          every so often at night
Tragic keys turn in the gates,
And specters of unknown
               recollections
Rise through the rattle of night planes.

The shattered window of a forgotten school
Will shine in the heart of the city—or maybe it's a cathedral.
Or the squares of shattered streets,
Or the clearings of winter forests...
And from the sky
Choirs of frail tender voices sing old lullabies from above
As well as the first words of lifeless children's primers.

...Нічні літаки пролітають далеко,
Лишаючи видива дивні,
        сріблисті,

Неначе за ними в шинелях солдатських,
В концтабірних куртках,
        лахмітті жіночім —
О ні! у ясному святковім вбранні! —
Колони дитячі,
        дитя за дитям...
Призначення, зміст?
        Просто — образ життя
Опівночі, в час літаків фіалкових...

...Night planes fly past far off in the distance,
Leaving strange silver
                    specters,

As though beyond them in soldiers' overcoats,
In concentration camp jackets,
                    in women's rags—
Oh no! in bright holiday attire!
Columns of children,
                    child after child...
Destination, contents?
                    Simply a vision of life
At midnight, in the time of violet planes...

tr. Michael M. Naydan

255

ОЗЕРО КІНЕРЕТ

Hryhory Falkovych

Прозорого єврейського мотиву
Ми самотужки вчились восени
Там, де вода, не знаючи спротиву,
Підважує апостольські човни.

Там предок мій з Давидового роду
Напровесні, у спеку, у сльоту
Ходив серед мого ж таки народу
І намовляв на вічну доброту.

Опівдні нам і дня було замало,
Тут стежка пам'ята Ісусів слід...
А озеро бриніло і снівало.
Неначе й не було двох тисяч літ.

Не вірити йому було несила.
І не було до нього вороття.
А скрипка, віщий здогад майбуття,
Сміялася вона і голосила,
І обіцяла — як саме життя.

LAKE CHINNERETH[1]

by Hryhory Falkovych

In autumn we were studying
A pellucid Hebrew motif
In a place where the water knows no resistance,
And lifts the apostles' boats.

There my ancestor from David's lineage
Walked among my people
In the early spring, in heat and foul weather,
Prodding them onto the path of eternal goodness.

At noon there wasn't enough daylight for us,
Here the path recalls Jesus's tracks...
And the lake strummed and sang,
As though it had not been two thousand years.

It was beyond my power not to believe it.
Yet there was no returning to it.
And a violin, a prophetic conjecture of the future,
Laughed and wailed,
And promised—like life itself.

tr. Michael M. Naydan

---

according to a note by Falkovych, the name of the 13-mile long, pear-shaped lake comes from the word "kinnor" (meaning "violin"). I am ...eful to Baruch Halpern for confirming for me that the Hebrew word means "harp-shaped" or "lyre-shaped." It is known as Lake of ...nesaret or the Sea of Galilee in the Bible. It goes by the name of Gennesar in Josephus. The contemporary name is Bahr Tabariyeh— ... of Tiberius. Because of its location amid mountains with dramatic temperature changes, the lake is known for quickly forming ...pestuous storms.

ЗОЛОТАВИЙ СОНЕТ
(В СТАРОМУ КИЄВІ)

Attila Mohylny

У тиші цих плавких провулків
луш сонце зблискує на вікнах
і кроків майже непомітна
луна — мов кошеняти муркіт.

Манірна мрійновтома квітня,
дахи — легкі, як поцілунки,
і сміх відлунюється лунко
у шатрах простору блакитних.

Стираються повільно грані,
все — позолота перетворень,
і гнучкість спалахів срібляних
в прозорій чаші водозбору.

І тільки музика, що тане
в меланхолійних стінах двору.

A GOLD-BEARING SONNET
(In Old Kiev)

by Attila Mohylny

In the silence of these placid alleys
with just the sun shining on the windows
and the nearly unnoticeable echo
of footsteps—like the purring of a kitten.

The mannered weary fancy of April,
rooftops—light as kisses,
and laughter echoing sonorously
in the azure tents of space.

Embers slowly disappear,
all is the gold of transformations
and the pliancy of silver flashes
in the translucent chalice of the basin.

It is just music drowning
in the melancholy walls of the yard.

tr. Michael Naydan

ФАНТАЗІЯ МЕТРО

Viktor Neborak

Зникає відображення ти знову
сам у собі як вертикаль незрима
сповільнює розігяану основу
геометричний простір за дверима
ти рухаешся в напрямку проміння
в юрбі по механічному тунелю
крізь погляди слова і сновидіння
цей рух не в небо втеча не в пустелю
у кола здеформовані і грані
у пошуки рослинної любові
твоє життя — це прожилки кленові
такі прозорі і тонкі у травні
і вертикаль що з небом поєднала
найглибші надра де часів немає
і око в небесах намалювала
блукаючий твій погляд піднімає

METRO FANTASY

by Viktor Neborak

The reflection disappears again you
in yourself are like an invisible vertical line
geometric space beyond the doors
slows down the scattered foundation
you move in the direction of a beam of light
along a mechanical tunnel in a throng
everywhere glances words and dreams
this movement is not to the sky escape not to a wasteland
borders deformed into circles
into searchings for herbal love
your life — these are veins of a maple
so translucent and thin in May
and the vertical line that fused with the sky
the deepest wombs where there is no time
and you painted an eye in the heavens
lifting up your wandering gaze

tr. Michael M. Naydan

ДОСИТЬ

Victoria Stakh

Досить.
Не думай про мене.
Пальці відштовхуються від ручки.
Очі відштовхуються від літер.
Різнойменним зарядом
лише телефонний диск.
Чуєш?
Не думай про мене.
Заглушується годинник.
Єдине слово добу відлічує.
Що робиш з моєю мовою?
. . . . любий . . . . любий . . . .
. . . .
. . . . любий . . . .

ENOUGH

by Victoria Stakh

Enough.
Don't think about me.
Fingers push away the pen.
Eyes push away the letters.
The phone is the only
neutral zone.
You hear that?
Don't think about me.
The clock turns mute.
Only words track the passing of time.
What are you doing to my language?
. . . . baby . . . . .dear . . . . . .
. . . .
. . . . heart . . . .

tr. Virlana Tkacz and Wanda Phipps

ОДА МОЗКОВІ

Victoria Stakh

Мій мозок — болющий.
Мій мозок — у м'язах.
Мій мозок у натовпі міцно ув'язнув.
Мій мозок — постійно сколошканий вулик.
Мій мозок літа між балконами вулиць.
Самотній.
       У місті.
          Без дівки.
             Без кисню.
Він вже на білизняній шворці повиснув.
Його вже під праску кладе господиня.
Можливо, хоч в цьому згодиться людині
      ...мій мозок...
      ...мій світ...
      ...інтелект мій і розум...
      ...мій... натовпний розум...
      ...мій...

          ...шворковий...
          ...розум...

ODE TO THE BRAIN

by Victoria Stakh

My brain's in pain.
My brain's a clenched muscle.
My brain's stuck in the crowd.
My brain's an angry beehive.
My brain flies between the balconies on the block.
Alone.
    In the city.
        No gal.
            No oxygen.
It's been hung out to dry on the clothes line.
And the housekeeper is about to iron it.
Maybe, now it will be of some use
           ...my brain...
           ...my world...
           ...my intellect and mind...
           ...my... mass mind...
           ...my

                ...strung out...
                ...brain...

tr. Virlana Tkacz and Wanda Phipps

БЛЮЗ

Ludmyla Taran

Рухами, жестами
      виліплюю лінії музики,
Підперті нитками голосу,
      навскісним промінням,
Плавною пороллю звуків,
      яка набігає згори.
Левада радості
Заростає струмистою зеленню.
І, мерехка, гойдлива,— тихо несе
      мене.
Синкопи смутку і жаги водночас.
І вуха повні зустрічного вітру.
...Вибрести із нестерпного лісу
      людей,
Зірвати ошийник, надсади —
      не дамся!
... Розпадиста сальва — о цей
      саксофон мерехтливий!
І вимислива мелодія лащиться,
      треться о серце.
Ласка на ласку, жадаю роздати її,
      що прибуває.
...Встигнути кожен може
      збожеволіти з болю
      і крику.
Синедріон дрімає — ти ж
      бо живи!
Вічноголодне серце здерло прокляту
      маску —
Яке ж бо воно беззахисне і бліде!
...Як я люблю заглядати в сумну
      оркестрову яму:

THE BLUES

by Ludmyla Taran

My movements, gestures
        form lines of music
Held up by threads of sound,
        a downpour of light,
Sprouting tones
        from above.
A meadow
Overgrown green with joy.
The web of sound lulls me, carries me
        away.
Melancholy syncopated by desire.
I let the wind fill my ears.
...Find my way out of the impenetrable forest
        of people
Break the chain around my neck, struggle,
        I won't give up.
The gleaming saxophone bursts forth.
The intricate melody caresses me,
        rubs up against the heart
Caress after caress, I want to pass on
        what has come to me.
...Anyone would
        go crazy from the pain
        and the crying.
The Sanhedrin dozes—but not
        I.
The ever-hungry heart tears off the damned
        disguise—
Now defenseless and pale.
...I love to look into the empty
        orchestra pit:

Тільки стільці і пульти —
           тайна іще дріма.
Кров же тремтить і хоче —
           ось я розповиваюсь
Ось я ліплю мелодію,
           що ліпить мене сама.

Only stools and music stands—
                    the mystery still asleep.
Then trembling with desire—
                    I start to unravel.
This is where I form the melody
                    that alone forms me.

tr. Virlana Tkacz and Wanda Phipps

РОЗЛИТА ЧОРНА ТУШ

Ludmyla Taran

Розлита чорна туш — красива:
Вона округла і м'яка,
Мов оксамит. Вологий полиск
Окреслює лежаче тіло
Об'ємно, тепло.
          Я люблю
У чорному — багатозначність:
І сум, і жах, і жаль, і пристрасть,
Що надить урвищем.
          Дивись:
Ніде ні натяку на ласку
На звабу, обіцяння шалу —
Суцільна строгість.
          Та з пітьми —
Хто хоче — той почує клич
Її урочистого серця.

INDIA INK

by Ludmyla Taran

The spot of India ink is beautifully
Round and seems soft
As velvet. Its moist sheen
Defines a reclining body
Giving it volume and heat.
     I love
Black—the multiplicity of its meanings:
Sorrow, fear, grief, passion
And the pull of the abyss.
     Look:
There is no fawning,
Frivolity, or frenzy—
Total rigor.
     But from this darkness
Those who want—hear the call of
A magnificent heart.

tr. Virlana Tkacz and Wanda Phipps

271

Ludmyla Taran
Ukraine

Oksana Zabuzhko
Ukraine

АВТОПОРТРЕТ БЕЗ РЕВНОЩІВ

Oksana Zabuzhko

Благословляю жінку, що на світанку відслонить
Вікна в твоєму домі.
Її вимита шкіра ряхтітиме холодом,
Як розтяте вранішнє яблуко.
Жінку, яка безшелесно, навшпиньках
Пройде на кухню,
Поставить каву.
Її очі і руки будуть при цьому сміятись.
Благословляю цю жінку,
Сонну птаху її волосся,
Затамований подих її ходи,
Сірника, що горить між пальців,
Роздвоюючись у безоднях зіниць,
Повільну блакитну музику вен
На руці, піднятій з гребенем...

Благословляю жінку, яку я тобі дарую,
Жінкуи якій належить пильнувати твій добрий ранок.
Це я відливаю її для тебе
Зі слів ясних, аж пекучих,
Що по краплі стікають поверхнею шибки,
В яку дивлюся,
І в її глибині коливається
Підводна квітка мого обличчя...
Благословляю цю жінку—як усе-таки шкода,
Що цієї жінки тобі ніколи не знати.

SELF-PORTRAIT WITHOUT THE JEALOUSIES

by Oksana Zabuzhko

I treasure the woman who at dawn
Opens the windows in your home,
Her washed skin sparkling with cold
Like an early ripe apple split in two.
The woman who silently on tiptoes
Will shuffle to the kitchen
To put on the coffee.
Her eyes and hands will smile on her way.
I treasure this woman,
The sleepy bird's nest of her hair,
The halting breadth of her gait,
A match burning between fingers
Doubling in the infinite abysses of her eyes,
The slow azure music of the veins
On her hand, raised high in the air with a comb...

I treasure the woman whom I bestow to you,
The woman who must take care of your good morning.
Here I pour her for you
From bright—even scalding—words,
That drip by drop flow off the top of the pane,
I gaze into her,
And in her depth the underwater flower
Of my face sways...
I revere this woman—though it's too bad
You'll never know her.

tr. Michael Nayden

THE BLUE HERON

Bjo Ashwill

There was this moment, you see.
I saw a Blue Heron.
The Blue Heron Moment.
This was the 24,703,200th moment
Of my life.

I saw a tall legged
Long necked, fat bodied blue bird.
Well, actually, that's not what I saw.
I saw God, or me, and the wind
Ruffling the Blue's feathers gently.

That moment,
The Blue Heron Moment,
Was framed in blue.
Shades of blue
A circular frame of sky and wind danced
Water. A new moon of water tucked
Between the marsh grass covered land
A sandwich of Blue Heron fishing for
Her lunch.

I sat, encased in my metal van
Sat, encased in my metal chair,
I, in my soft living skin, surrounded with
Sweaters, scarves and hats, sat.

I saw through my eyes, through the window glass,
Through the noises of my brain, through the wind,
Through the reflections refracting on
This world I feel and see but do not
Know.

I saw the grace of the moment.
The amazing grace of the Blue Heron Moment
As she turned and saw me, you see.
She turned and she saw me.

My hands convulsed around the camera.
Knowing she would move. Leave. The moment
Shatters into another moment. Still —
I must have this moment on film
To carry, to see, to remember — silly me —
But I am not a Blue Heron — yet.

I opened the side door with a motor grinding sound
My wheelchair lift groaned itself out, like a
Drawbridge over a moat. My chair whines out
To the tip of the lift and I sigh,
"She stays — she stays" in wonder that this moment,
The grace of this moment, still lives.
Despite me. Despite my compulsive greed —
The amazing grace of the Blue Heron Moment stays.

She didn't miss a beat, fluid movement blended
One into the other. She cocked her head, shifted her
Weight slowly from one knobby knee to the other,
Bent, nipped at the water and then lifting
Her long neck she swallowed silver morsels of fish.
The wind stroked her feathers like a careless
Hand. The same wind that brushed my face
In passing.

She turned and in silhouette, I saw
Two herons, one reflected in the water,
Mirror image. Two curves, two circles
Two s-shaped necks balancing
The Yin and the Yang of the moment.
I was complete. It all fit.

Then she turned toward me and lifted her
Long thin neck and looked at me.
We looked at each other as the wind
Passed us in yet another world wide circle.
We simply looked at each other.
And then I know — what — I do not know,
But I knew, then and there, here and now
Something.

Something about circles, something about moments,
Something about peace and being.
I tucked the Blue Heron Moment,
Into my heart.
I take it out and feel it —
On rainy days — when a Blue Heron
Comes in handy.
When a Blue Heron looks at me and
We are the Universe.

Elizabeth Bartlett
United States

THE BULLET BALLET

Elizabeth Bartlett

We're not thick-skinned enough
and bullet-truth vests have yet to be invented.
The shots can be random, accidental or direct,
all catch you unaware and can prove lethal.
They leave holes, burns, lesions, scars
in the eyes, the throat, the heart, the mind.
Bullet truths. We gasp at the shock,
the absolute reality. We feel exposed
as our nerves quiver and recoil. So hard
to get used to the ping, the sting,
the sensation of being ripped apart.
We need truth-proof armor
like the knights in old days.
From whatever hand of friend or stranger,
parent, lover, child or idol,
the unexpected shot assails our innocence,
suddenly transparent as thin glass
which cracks, splinters, shatters.

Truth hurts, you say?
Ah to be bullet proof to human facts!
Listen to children's cries,
the first signs come too early.
Listen to old people's groans,
the last signs come too late.
No wonder we are attracted to monsters,
huge, fierce, so well protected
by gigantic claws and teeth,
bristling plates and tough hides.

How beautiful to be so ugly,
a beast stuffed with final truth.
On guard! Be quick! To turn, to dodge, to leap
the careless word, the indifferent shrug,
the ignorant, selfish, vengeful aim. You need
practice to endure and survive the bullet ballet.
So on your toes, flex, kick, whirl,
and let the shots fire away.

THE CENTENARIAN

Elizabeth Bartlett

My age, you ask. I find it hard to say.
The same inner voice, the same inner eye —
surely you understand. It's like one's name.
Do the years change it? I've been answering
to mine since I was born — at home, in school,
at play. How soon we get to know that I
means oneself, whether hungry, happy, sad...
What else is childhood, if not me and I?
Then curiosity got me — you know,
adolescence. Well, and what did I find?
That there were other selves, as well as mine,
and each as self-important as can be.
How the outside boundaries of the world
expand, when the ego cracks its cocoon!
Goodbye, old familiar! Hello, new strange!
And off I went, now fearful then brave,
searching for that special affinity.
What an adventure — in daylight shadows,
in moonlight forest, daring the unknown!
I was a butterfly, a flutterby,
all through that fumbling season we call youth.
Finally, much like the sleeping princess,
I woke up one day and I was nineteen.
Now *that's* the best age for a girl to be,
when she is young enough to be attractive
and yet old enough to be considered
thoughtful and responsible, shall we say?
Able, at least, to take care of herself
and be qualified as a person, yes.

Which I was, since I earned my own money,
made my own decisions, and had to take
the consequences! As Voltaire put it,
I was cultivating my own garden.
Unfortunately, mine had plenty of weeds.
A foolish heart only thinks of roses
and has no mind for aphids, thorns or blight.
Oh well, it did not break my heart or back,
much as I strained both, for I was as strong
as a girl in love can be. When I think
of the energy and confidence
it takes to make mountains into molehills
and oases out of deserts, I swear
a girl in love can perform miracles.
"Surely the water tastes like vintage wine?"
"Dear Lazarus lover, you can not die!"
So nineteen I remained for a long time,
since the everpresent stretched before me
like a bridge, one that never seemed to end.
How I ran and ran to escape the years!
It was one island after another,
surrounded by atolls and heavy seas.
By thirty-nine I grew somewhat resigned
to living, to the utter black and white
of yes and no — yet stubborn to admit
its gray, that mediocre in-between
of nagging tongues, thick waists and weary sighs.
Forgive me, I wanted adventure, not
security! Rather a hummingbird
than a mud turtle, you know what I mean?
Stay put and the world comes to a standstill.
I knew that. And with all there was to see,
I needed wings. That's when I decided
to make them from the feathers in my nest.

By then I had collected quite a few
from marsh and shore, lagoon and upland ground,
from raptor, crane, exotic visitor —
I perched, waded and climbed cliffs to make my wings!
A strange bird, no doubt, but one determined
to fly — and I did, I did. I traveled
everywhere, an attractive thirty-nine
for decades. Well, why not? So much, you see,
depends on how you think and feel. Birthdays —
good heavens, what do they mean to the stars?
You look surprised. Ah yes, to develop
a time sense sometimes takes to fifty-nine.
It wasn't easy, believe me. Of course
there were the signs — not inside, not at all —
but there were those gray hairs and telling lines,
as usual — and most of all, the way
people look at you when they talk to you.
Now that can age you more than years! Until
you begin to doubt the sound of your voice
and the look in your eyes, as though you changed
into someone else with a different name
once you turned sixty-nine. Which is nonsense!
No matter, I refused to be deceived.
Some people are born old, have you noticed?
While others — well, I think of violins
that look and sound as well at seventy-nine
as at eighty-nine. Yes, and any room
can be a concert hall, with your own ear
as audience — if you make a career
of living, instead of dying. And when
I needed applause, what could be better
than the ocean's waves, the wind in the trees?
Why, they grow even louder with the years!
It's simply a matter of listening,
don't you agree? So when you ask my age,
I could say nineteen or nine and ninety —
it all depends on how I feel and think!

CRY "PLAGUE!"
(To *The Living* by Anthony Clarvoe)

Elizabeth Bartlett

Sarah, we have our own plague,
a different kind of plague
but a plague, nevertheless.
Yours reported 1000 cases a month,
then every week, every day,
every hour... and lost count.

We know the dangers.   The air
breathes infection. Yet we
persist — and grieve. Our loss
is more than faith: our friends,
burials, dying hopes. Like cracks
in our bell hearts. Strangers
surround us. We swallow bullets.

We need to be tied — wrists, ankles.
Especially the children.
In their fever, they infect others,
they break bonds, form gangs,
and run in the streets. Dogs
and taxes do not help. The plague
is out of control.

Our kennels are no longer safe.
The jungle has invaded them,
as our scripts, films and
dinosaur bones reveal. Drums
beat a steady tempo, with loud
songs, shrieks and pounding feet.
Also, we play games, and who wins
has to last, to laugh. To fall
is not funny, even for rotting apples.

Hold on or let go. One has to know
to what. Otherwise
cry "Plague! Keep away! Don't touch!"

LATE OCTOBER, SAN DIEGO, CALIFORNIA

Elizabeth Bartlett

My eyes erase the car lights
and invite the sunset in.
My eyes blot out the streets,
houses, shops, buildings
and replace them with trees,
bushes, wild grass, weeds.

I blink and the canyon sends up
a whiff of skunk. Gophers
lift the dust, ravens
comb the twilight, and a fox
lopes downtrail to a creek.

The sky still gleams wide miles
across the bay. The past
is present and slowly sinks
behind it. Because day's arc
is shorter, the dusk is brief.
Silence draws a curtain
of sleep over nests and burrows.

Signs, windows, lamp posts
dot the land again.
Bridges beckon the night's islands
to shore like ships.
My eyes reshape the hour
to this here and now.

Was I there? Was I then?

OLD MAP, NEW MAP

Elizabeth Bartlett

Where is the street that walled me in
with witches, ghosts and bogeymen,
who haunted me with warnings of
what would happen if I didn't watch out?
where it was only safe to play under a tent
made of sheets behind the piano
or inside the bathtub while mama watched.
You mean that street is gone, is part
of a freeway for interurban traffic?

Where is the park across from the school
which was used as a playground
once you stopped sucking your thumb,
wetting your bed, and wondering
where you went while you slept?
And if it snowed, there were sleds
on which to belly-whop and shout *gangway*.
Now the only park is a park-ing lot
between a bank and a cheap hotel.

What happened to the mountain I climbed,
hoping to find a shortcut home
while it was still light? I remember
slippery paths along jagged cliffs
that dropped to wild ravines and dark
tunnels with no help in sight.
It shrinks imagination to call that hill
of weeds and holes the massif of
my journey towards the future.

And I know there was a river, too,
which took me years to get across,
aware of roaring falls far from shore
with nothing to cling to
or save me from drowning.
Now a meandering stream upstate
crossed by several bridges,
not bad for fishing, they say,
even a swimming hole or two.

POSTED FROM COLIMA

Elizabeth Bartlett

It is not the physical fact of being here.
I can explain that:
a tropical village, surrounded by fields of sugarcane,
its 13,000 ft. volcano against the sky,
the cobbled streets, adobe walls and tiled roofs
enclosing their quota of chickens, pigs and goats,
with children in all sizes happy to be together,
while pure white butterflies silently clap wings...

I could list all kinds of facts of eye and ear,
and other senses, too:
like the smell of lime trees in the rain,
or the taste of wild mint and soft pink pulp of figs,
or fingering spider lilies alongside rocks and pools,
the feel of the wind off pine slopes or up from the sea,
the rocking trot on a burro, the nudging gait on a horse,
while the canebrake snaps and bends to either side...

But how explain a friendship with the morning,
the joy of meeting it
across miles of open country through my windows,
inviting it in to breakfast for the latest news,
taking a walk with it to exchange smiles and greetings,
sharing each other's thoughts, moods, errands,
as we lead the day like a cow to pasture,
until it is noon — and must we part already?

And how explain the peace of afternoon,
when life withdraws
and time comes to a standstill in the heat,
when nothing seems to move except the silence,
its shadow slowly filtering through the hills,
until a breeze announces another resurrection
with the barking of dogs and the opening of doors,
as the whole village awakes refreshed once more?

Or how explain a love affair with the night,
the waiting eagerness,
having bathed and dressed and prepared its welcome
with fresh-cut flowers, Bach's Prelude in C Minor,
a tray set out with iced drinks and tasty tidbits,
while the sky flames behind the volcano
for one more long embrace, before extinguishing the light
in a sweet surrender to philosophy, poetry, and art?

SAFE EXIT

Elizabeth Bartlett

A cold wind blows.

It comes from the breath of men
who have talked with the dead.
It carries the lash of their tongues
against the living.
It burns with the icy fire
that rages in their eyes.
It pummels the air with their fists
to bruise our flesh and bones.

We recoil.
We cringe.
An icicle trickles down our spine.
We huddle inside our skin.
It is impossible to keep warm.
It is unbearable to stand still.
Conscience freezes.
Memory cracks.

Automatons,
we move in an interior arctic
of ghostly anonymity,
seeking an exit.

Only the fog
can help us to escape
after the fall,
before the winter.
It walls out the world.
It envelops us.
Within the fog
we resume our identity.

Obscure.
Comfortable.
Our own breath grows warm
as voices blur
and eyes fade.
There is no wind.
The cold cannot reach us
in our smoke-filled cave.

Far off
a siren shrieks disaster.
Far off — as we move
farther and farther away.

We are alive, separate, safe.

"Journey's End" is a twelve-tone poem, the last poem
in Elizabeth Bartlett's last book of poetry, *Around the
Clock* (Laurinburg, N.C.: St. Andrews's Press 1989).
As she wished, it was read to her when she was dying,
and again when her ashes were cast upon the sea.

JOURNEY'S END

Elizabeth Bartlett

A lost ship
I moor in the shelter of your arms

And hold close
with frayed rope, torn sail and leaning mast.

Dependent
on wind, chance and my own woman's strength

I have voyaged
far and long from point of origin

To this port,
the safe, blessed haven of no return.

Now keep me
content to dream, at peace on the shore.

A HISTORY OF NAVIGATION

Nancy Eimers

1. INSOMNIA

Awake at midnight on the factory side of town,
I swear the only thing I haven't tried

is counting ships. The Water Witch, the Golden Fleece,
the Silver Wake, the Sailor Boy, the Morning Star,

and last, the Kalamazoo. I made that up. This shipwrecked town—
I can almost *see* its rooftops fathoms down.

I think the starless night is trying to push
right through the walls of this house.

So is the screaming train en route through our backyard
with a load of dark that would fill up Lake Michigan.

Streetlight pours through a flowering rent
on a sheet that curtains our bedroom window;

my sleeping husband is another window
dark for hours now, and I am watching him,

too far out to care for signs and omens:
the traffic light blinks red and red and red;

the Minute Market, lit inside, shuts off.
I call it Murder Market; someone was shot there once.

How can he sleep through the dirty sound?
Garage bands never sleep. The singer's voice

is husky, dragged through mud.
Just one way to tell a love story.

Not our story, in particular,
or his. The story of an open mouth.

*

Mouth opens, breathing quietly,
you seem to skim over the water, as a ship does.
How can you sleep?
Halfway down the street, a man is laughing,
so hard I think he'll empty out,
but no, the laugh goes on.
It just gets fainter down the street.
Once the last remembered house blinks out
it's all dead reckoning,
whimsy or currents, wind, a lazy minutehand
as I think my way past any hope of sleep.
This afternoon—what was I screaming right into your eyes?
Poor Richard's Diner down the street
will be dark until morning, ages away,
though in my mind I am already groping
for landmarks:

Oh red and blue town of Statler Cement,
Kozel Iron & Metal, oh Dairy Mart,
oh corner of Crosstown Parkway and Mill
with your two orange newspaper machines,
the Detroit Free Press and the Kalamazoo Gazette—
my mind is newsprint letters cut out of a page of night.
Will things we said leave holes in our morning and afternoon?

2. THE WORST FIGHT IN OUR HISTORY

After a squall, on the beach from Ludington
to Sleeping Bear Point,
the breakers push and drag ashore
the timbers to a hundred ancient wrecks.
Floating stairways. A stove-in pilot house.

When the part of us that feels most alive
rises through the fathoms of the argument,
we look around, we ask how far
our voices carry us.

Did the neighbors hear?
Your face empties out like a room for rent.

February 4: auspicious day for marriage
and repair of ships.

What can we do for each other? Out the window,
across the oceanic lawn
I see a neighbor turning busily away
from the mouth of our quiet
to *his* lawn and *his* flowerbed and *his* house and *his* quiet—

*

—after the age of schooners, after the age of steamers
after the walking-beam engine and the paddlewheel
with good power on the downstroke

but not much on the up,
in the sickening lunges of smoke and pause,
how can anyone have much of an appetite?

But everyone seems to be ravenous.
In the morning a diner is mostly men and smoke,
men who blow out smoke in stale blossomings,

297

blue anchors, stale hearts drifting apart—
men whose stares dribble nowhere.
How many ages ago did I see a face as if through wavy glass?

What day was it, what time, whose face?

I want to make a date with your sleeping face.
Tomorrow morning. You and me
our greasy eggs and American fries.
We'll tell our dreams
though probably not quiet *to* each other's eyes.
Let each one sail his lack of narrative
as if there were a port
in all that fog.
Or will I have slept enough to dream?
Sleepless nights blink red in the window,
morning is an empty parking lot.

I want to ask your face across the fish-tank of a booth:
whose name is advertised on the coffee cups
floating toward us on a tray?
Is it yours or mine?
Which one of us is Kozel, Statler, Crosstown, Mill?
Poor Richard will be wiping the counter
the way he always does,
between the booths there will be those troughs
where it gets all quiet
after the gale-wind blows
for the early shift. Across the silences
of dollar bills tucked under plates
I will remember this
dream about owls up in the trees.
They are screeching
here I am.

3. A HISTORY OF NAVIGATION

Sometimes in a squall
the pouring of storm oil on the water
doesn't work. Then the wind goes whistling
over the forty- and fifty-foot crests
and the gloomy cook goes sloshing around in the ship's galley
stacking pots and pans on the highest shelf.
Each time
we turn the volume up, then down, behind the words,
we weep, we make of sweet relief our peace,
we scan the windows for superlatives: *One of the most daring*
pieces of expert seamanship
in the history of navigation!
To voyage over water, to make our way—
let's lie in bed in the hour of shipwrecked laughs,
one awake and one asleep,
and steer past the first or last
jalopy backfiring in the alley.

Poor car, poor town,
roar down inside us and sleep.

A NIGHT WITHOUT STARS

Nancy Eimers

And the lake was a dark spot
                  on a lung.
Some part of its peace was dead; the rest was temporary. Sleeping ducks
           and geese,
goose shit underfoot
                and wet gray blades of grass.
The fingerlings like sleeping bullets
                          hung deep in the troughs of the hatchery
and cold traveled each one end to end,
such cold,
      such distances.

We lay down in the grass on our backs—
beyond the hatchery the streetlights were mired in fog and so
there were no stars,
                or stars would say there was no earth.

Just a single homesick firefly lit on a grass blade.
Just our fingers
                curled and clutching grass,
this dark our outmost hide, and under it
                        true skin.

BALLOONS

Dolores Guglielmo

The child in me whispered, "Do it!"
I bought them at the
   Stationery Store
Where helium breathed life
   Into rubber spheres
   Of blue
      green
      red
      yellow
   Attached to pink lassoes
   All gathered together
   As they fought to rise
      Like a Phoenix—
         Releasing them to
            Soar higher and higher
            Into the wind—
Intangible slashes of color
   Dots on the horizon
Dappling cumulus
Ghostlike
   Disappearing behind
      Scudded apparitions—
Caressing the sun
My heart beating wildly
   With quickened energy...
      As the child in me whispered,

"Do it again!"

BLACK PICASSO

Dolores Guglielmo

Trains rumbling through maws
Dimly lit
Walls emblazoned with hieroglyphics
Of "Mark 370"
In flesh-torn slashes of blood-reds
And oozing yellows
He was there—
He was everywhere
In the littered entrails
Of the "Bronx Express"
"Brooklyn Downtown"
"Queens Local"
See him as he alights
With nimble feet
From train to train
He paints by twilight
A Black Picasso
In the graveyards of
Broken tenements
Broken dreams
Idling hours
Reborn in a foggy trainyard
Of stalled sidewinders
Deftly wielding paint can in hand
Venerable in vestment jeans
"Mark 370" was there!

From streamlining
To mainlining
In the rain soaked ground
Of "Archangels Cemetery"
Carved in limestone...
Here lies Mark "Booker" Jones
Born - 1970
Died - 1986
Oh yeah man!
He is there.

TRUCK TO CORNUCOPIA

Dolores Guglielmo

When the truck pulled up to the wooden
    framed house
Papa yelled, "Get the kids in the back!"
Mama screamed, "But how are we gonna get
    them all to fit?"
Papa remonstrated, "Now Mama, we'll get 'em
    all in!"
First Peter, then Jo, Ellen, Richard, Arthur,
    Maggie, Concetta, Tom and Joseph.
We screeched and hollered as children do —
Careening along the highway
In an open truck...
All standing on our toes
To see everything there was to see.
It was three miles to Long Island City
Where licorice sticks belched soot,
And tired factory workers
Peered from blackened, broken windows.
It was a great rambling building,
Rain-streaked with cracked powdered brick...
N.R.A. banners gliding lazily in the hot sun.
The sign on the building read: "Department of
    Welfare–Clothing Division"
Papa screamed excitedly, "Alright kids, everybody
    down!"
Mama looked on worriedly, as each child jumped
    from the truck—
She measured the children for shoes,
With a long string;
As we then walked down long aisles of cotton
    dresses, underwear and shoes.

The boys shrieked with delight as they tried on
      bulky denims, and thick cotton shirts.
When we were through, we piled back into the truck,
Waving our new shoes at passersby along the 59th
      Street Bridge,
Sniffing the new leather, pressing them dearly to
      our faces.

"A BEARD FOR A BLUE PANTRY"

Donald Hall

In Alice Mattison's dream
I have written a new poem I call
"A Beard for a Blue Pantry."

My wife Jane has leukemia
and I sit by her painful bed
as petechiae bloom on her skin

and white cells proliferate.
The summer after we married
I grew a black beard, and Jane

wrote a poem on the airplane
flying home from California:
"First Eight Days of the Beard."

A dozen years later I shaved
that curly intractable beard
when it turned as white

as King Arthur in the pantry
where Bluebeard the cat
birdwatched from the breadbox.

In those deliberate days,
Jane made bread so honest,
once it went blue in the pantry

on a hot August weekend.
Each morning I brought her coffee
in bed, and we worked together

apart, Jane over the kitchen
at her desk making poems
until the dew dried and she mulched

her roses. Or she fed chickadees
blackoil sunflower seed, or walked
the dog, or answered Alice's letter,

or washed abundant hair
that is gone now, like Bluebeard
whose sick young eyes glazed over.

THE HUNTERS

Donald Hall

In the cold mist of the November
morning, pickups park deep
in fallen leaves while hunters
file singly into the woods,
looking for deer that browse
in abandoned apple orchards
by cellar holes. God watches
them move under hemlock and oak
like fleas in a dog's pelt,
so many of them, tiny among
the trees. As the heretic said,
"It makes no difference, a
thousand angels or one:
There is no number in eternity."

THE PORCELAIN COUPLE

Donald Hall

When Jane felt well enough for me to leave her
for a whole day, I drove south by the river
to empty my mother Lucy's house in Connecticut.
I hurried from room to room, cellar to attic,
opening a crammed closet, then turning
to discover a chest with five full drawers.
I labelled for shipping sofas and chairs,
bedroom sets, and tables; I wrapped figurines
and fancy teacups in paper, preserving things
she cherished—and dreaded, in her last years,
might go for a nickel on the Spring Glen lawn.
Everywhere I looked I saw shelves and tabletops
covered with Lucy's glass animals and music boxes.
Everywhere in closets, decades of dresses hung
in dead air. I carried garbage bags in one hand,
and with the other swept my mother's leftover
possessions into sacks for the Hamden dump.
I stuffed bags full of blouses, handkerchiefs,
and the green-gold dress she wore to Bermuda.
At the last moment I discovered and saved
a cut-glass tumbler, stained red at the top,
Lucy 1905 scripted on the stain. In the garage
I piled the clanking bags, then drove four hours
north with my hands tight on the Honda's wheel,
drank a beer looking through Saturday's mail,
pitched into bed beside Jane fitfully asleep,
and woke exhausted from rolling unendable
nightmares of traffic and fire. In my dreams
I grieved or mourned interchangeably for Lucy,
for Lucy's things, for Jane and for me.

When I woke, I rose as if from a drunken sleep
after looting a city and burning its temples.
All day as I ate lunch or counted out pills,
or as we lay weeping, hugging in bed together,
I counted precious things from our twenty years:
a blue vase, a candelabrum Jane carried on her lap
from the Baja, and the small porcelain box
from France I found under the tree one Christmas
where a couple in relief stretch out asleep,
like a catafalque, on the pastel double bed
of the box's top, both wearing pretty nightcaps.

WEEDS AND PEONIES

Donald Hall

Your peonies burst out, white as snow squalls,
with red flecks at their shaggy centers,
in your border of prodigies by the porch.
I carry one magnanimous blossom inside
to float in a glass bowl, as you used to do.

Ordinary happiness, remembered in sorrow,
blows like snow into the abandoned garden
to overcome daisies. Your blue coat
vanishes down Pond Road into imagined snowflakes
with Gus at your side, his great tail swinging,

but you will not return, tired and satisfied,
and sorrow's repeated particles suffuse the air—
like the dog yipping through the entire night,
or the cat stretching awake, then curling
to dream of her mother's milky nipples.

A raccoon dislodges a geranium from its pot.
Flowers, roots, and dirt lie upended
in the back garden, where lilies begin
their daily excursions above stone walls
in the season of old roses. I pace beside weeds

and snowy peonies, staring at Mount Kearsarge
where you climbed wearing purple hiking boots.
"Hurry back. Be careful, climbing down."
Your peonies lean their vast heads westward
as if they might topple. Some topple.

Donald Justice
United States

PANTOUM OF THE GREAT DEPRESSION

Donald Justice

Our lives avoided tragedy
Simply by going on and on,
Without end and with little apparent meaning.
Oh, there were storms and small catastrophes.

Simply by going on and on
We managed. No need for the heroic.
Oh, there were storms and small catastrophes.
I don't remember all the particulars.

We managed. No need for the heroic.
There were the usual celebrations, the usual sorrows.
I don't remember all the particulars.
Across the fence, the neighbors were our chorus.

There were the usual celebrations, the usual sorrows
Thank god no one said anything in verse.
The neighbors were our only chorus,
And if we suffered we kept quiet about it.

At no time did anyone say anything in verse.
It was the ordinary pities and fears consumed us,
And if we suffered we kept quiet about it.
No audience would ever know our story.

It was the ordinary pities and fears consumed us.
We gathered on porches; the moon rose; we were poor.
What audience would ever know our story?
Beyond our windows shone the actual world.

We gathered on porches, the moon rose; we were poor.
And time went by, drawn by slow horses.
Somewhere beyond our windows shone the world.
The Great Depression had entered our souls like fog.

And time went by, drawn by slow horses.
We did not ourselves know what the end was.
The Great Depression had entered our souls like fog.
We had our flaws, perhaps a few private virtues.

But we did not ourselves know what the end was.
People like us simply go on.
We have our flaws, perhaps a few private virtues,
But is is by blind chance only that we escape tragedy.

And there is no plot in that; it is devoid of poetry.

HALLEY'S COMET

Stanley Kunitz

Miss Murphy in first grade
write its name in chalk
across the board and told us
it was roaring down the storm tracks
of the Milky Way at frightful speed
and if it wandered off its course
and smashed into the earth
there'd be no school tomorrow.
A red-bearded preacher from the hills
with a wild look in his eyes
stood in the public square
at the playground's edge
proclaiming he was sent by God
to save every one of us,
even the little children.
"Repent, ye sinners!" he shouted,
waving his hand-lettered sign.
At supper I felt sad to think
that it was probably
the last meal I'd share
with my mother and my sisters;
but I felt excited too,
and scarcely touched my plate.
So mother scolded me
and sent me early to my room.
The whole family's asleep now
except for me. They never heard me steal
into the stairwell hall and climb
the ladder to the fresh night air.

Look for me, Father, on the roof
of the red brick building
at the foot of Green Street—
that's where we live, you know, on the top floor.
I'm the boy in the white flannel gown
sprawled on the coarse gravel bed
searching the starry sky,
waiting for the world to end.

MY MOTHER'S PEARS

Stanley Kunitz

Plump, green-gold, Worcester's pride,
    transported through autumn skies
        in a box marked Handle With Care

sleep eighteen Bartlett pears,
    hand-picked and polished and packed
        for deposit at my door,

each in its crinkled nest
    with a stub of stem attached
        and a single bright leaf like a flag.

A smaller than usual crop,
    but still enough to share with me,
        as always at harvest time.

Those strangers are my friends
    whose kindness blesses the house
        my mother built at the edge of town

beyond the last trolley-stop
    when the century was young, and she
        proposed, for her children's sake,

to marry again, not knowing how soon
    the windows would grow dark
        and the velvet drapes come down.

Rubble accumulates in the yard,
    workmen are hammering on the roof,
        I am standing knee-deep in dirt

with a shovel in my hand.
>Mother has wrapped a kerchief round her head,
>>her glasses glint in the sun.

When my sisters appear on the scene,
>gangly and softly tittering,
>>she waves them back into the house

to fetch us pails of water,
>and they skip out of our sight
>>in their matching middy blouses.

I summon up all my strength
>to set the pear tree in the ground
>>unwinding its burlap shroud.

It is taller than I. "Make room
>for the roots!" my mother cries,
>"Dig the hole deeper."

CONSISTENCIES

William Olsen

The houses moving under the streetlights for the evening,
the shadow of a noon grasshopper
on the driveway,
first fireflies in a beginning rain,

how you've never seen a raindrop hit a firefly.

The cloud that crawls like a snail

up from the long ocean brooding over nothing—
it will murder us before we will murder it
over nothing—

but who has the heart to stop.

And how that cloud has a profile, Jesus
the outline of change is fresh upon it-how that
change can't let go.

That the executed mannequin consistencies
in all the little store windows
of America bare our inner light,
and the sky looking all out of sorts up there

like a regurgitated starling,

and the stars the connections the vacuums,
the quiz shows the families watch,
the dots the children connect,
the fish older than aquariums,
our criminals and their numbered stenciled numbers—

though to our futures living
beyond the blackening lawns
it comes to the same thing,

we are not in the world of the dead.

ON ECKHART AND A MOOSE

William Olsen

He would have been tried by his Church had he not had the good luck
    to die first.
He claimed the soul got younger all the time
and called the body an evening knowledge
and was convinced that when the angels knew creatures without God
    it became twilight.
But it is said by the feather that falls without the stellar jay—
even as that feather stops falling, even then it is said,
even though the burnt pines here hardly require jays—
that even he wondered how we would finally give our lives away
if no one particularly wanted them,
and wondered whether the merchants of death would ever burst
    with kindness.
Till we can hear teeth grind to speak more of these matters.
One face of evening to feed on all this sweet rot.
It believes its being will never be turned away.
Our optimism leaves them to come down freely from the volcanic ridge
and be in every way as driven as we were, and spend
their one life looking out of that life
waiting for the brutal facts to change.
The first tender shoots of arrowhead already
too far gone to go back, the dust on the dash
and on the dials of a dead radio of a used car
sparkled as residue too fine to wager.
This is what death likes, the little ice ages,
June, fresh snow, new aspen flocked with it,
primped white clouds of it impaled by branches or wedges
between twigs, asphalt's intestinal shine,
a pond to shine even late evening.

I think I could have heard my own death if I got
quiet enough and then I could hear the ecstatic profit
and laugh at the tactical glories
as its head laddered into the flowery phrases,
to vacuum clean both sweet and rotten while more lilies
        than could be mouthed
rode the bull's eye ripples, and ropes of water
streamed when the head pulled up, the eyes—
when this moment was full all time fell from us,
        or should have,
with all the goodbyes and the all vast brief mindfuls—
its face was dark—we didn't know what darkness was,
our flimsy consciences swept this way and that
through narrowing years and widening minutes.

Mona Van Duyn
United States

MR. AND MRS. JACK SPRAT IN THE KITCHEN

Mona Van Duyn

"About half a box,"
I say, and the male
weighs his pasta sticks
on our postal scale.

To support my sauce
of a guesswork rhymer
he boils by the laws
of electric timer.

Our joint creation,
my searchings, revisions,
tossed with his ration
of compulsive precisions,

so mimics life
we believe it mandated
that God had a wife
who collaborated.

And cracked, scraped, old,
still the bowl glows gold.

THE CONTEST
For the XXVIth Olympiad

Edd Wheeler

Mid-passage on the signal
Promontory this is
What the contest comes to:
Runners and the speckled sea
Of travelers expectant
At the gates. Braided hours whinny
For anthems and a chance
To arrest the bright trophies.
After the feast we engorge
The startled carnival.
Time eats us yet we stay
Hungry for the chase.

A BARRED OWL

Richard Wilbur

The warping night-air having brought the boom
Of an owl's voice into her darkened room,
We tell the wakened child that all she heard
Was an odd question from a forest bird,
Asking of us, if rightly listened to,
"Who cooks for you?" and then "Who cooks for you?"

Words, which can make our terrors bravely clear,
Can also thus domesticate a fear,
And send a small child back to sleep at night
Not listening for the sound of stealthy flight
Or dreaming of some small thing in a claw
Borne up to some dark branch and eaten raw.

A DIGRESSION

Richard Wilbur

Having confided to the heavy-lipped
Mailbox his great synoptic manuscript,
He stands light-headed in the lingering clang.
How lightly, too, he feels his briefcase hang!

And now it swings beside his knees, as they
From habit start him on his evening way,
With the tranced rhythm of a metronome,
Past hall and grove and stadium toward his home.

Yet as the sun-bathed campus slips behind,
A giddy lack of purpose fills his mind,
Making him swerve into a street which for
Two decades he has managed to ignore.

What stops him in his tracks is that his soul,
Proposing nothing, innocent of goal,
Sees no perspective narrowing between
Gold-numbered doors and frontages of green,

But for the moment as obstructive storm
Of specks and flashes that will take no form,
a roiled mosaic or a teeming scrim
That seems to have no pertinence to him.

It is his purpose now as, turning 'round,
He takes his bearings and is homeward bound,
To ponder what the world's confusion meant
When he regarded it without intent.

A WALL IN THE WOODS: CUMMINGTON

Richard Wilbur

1.

What is it for, now that dividing neither
Farm from farm nor field from field, it runs
Through deep impartial woods, and is transgressed
By boughs of pine or beech from either side?
Under that woven tester, buried here
Or there in laurel-patch or shrouding vine,
It is for grief at what has come to nothing,
What even in this hush is scarcely heard—
Whipcrack, the ox's lunge, the stoneboat's grating,
Work-shouts of young men stooped before their time
Who in their stubborn heads foresaw forever
The rose of apples and the blue of rye.
It is for pride, as well, in pride that built
With levers, tackle, and abraded hands
What two whole centuries have not brought down.
Look how with shims they made the stones weigh inward,
Binding the water-rounded with the flat;
How to a small ravine they somehow lugged
A long, smooth girder of a rock, on which
To launch their wall in air, and overpass
The narrow stream that still slips under it.
Rosettes of lichen decorate their toils,
Who labored here like Pharaoh's Israelites;
Whose grandsons left for Canaans in the west.
Except to prompt a fit of elegy
It is for us no more, or if it is,
It is a sort of music for the eye,
A rugged ground-bass like the bagpipe's drone
On which the leaf-light like a chanter plays.

2.

He will hear no guff
About Jamshyd's court, this small,
Striped, duff-colored resident
On top of the wall,

Who, having given
An apotropaic shriek
Echoed by crows in heaven,
Is off like a streak.

There is no tracing
The leaps and scurries with which
He braids his long castle, ra-
Cing, by gap, ledge, niche

And Cyclopean
Passages, to reappear
Sentry-like on a rampart
Thirty feet from here.

What is he saying
Now, in a steady chipping
Succinctly plucked and cadenced
As water dripping?

It is not drum-taps
For a lost race of giants,
But perhaps says something, here
In Mr. Bryant's

Homiletic woods,
Of the brave art of forage
And the good of a few nuts
In burrow-storage;

Of agility
That is not sorrow's captive,
Lost as it is in being
Briskly adaptive;

Of the plenum, charged
With one life through all changes,
And of how we are enlarged
By what estranges.

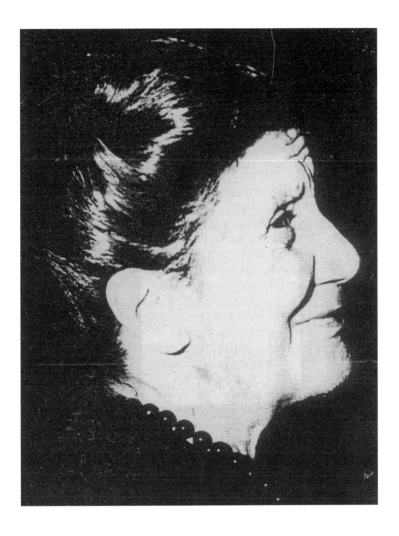

Desanka Maksimović
Yugoslavia

ПОТРЕБНО МИ ЈЕ

Desanka Maksimović

Потребно ми је много сунаца,
и то и ноћу,
једно да ме сусреће,
једно да за мном светлост баца,
у понору једно дубоком,
једно да носим у руци
кад од јада не видим прст пред оком.

Потребно ми је много нежности,
и то свакога дана,
и много од милоште речи;
потребно ми је примирје
између срца и сећања
између неба
и бола који пред њим клечи.

Потребна су ми добродошлицом озарена
лица многа,
и то свакога трена,
потребан ми пријатељ и то што већи,
потребни су ми мостови висећи
преко мржње,
преко неспоразума непремостивога.

I NEED

by Desanka Maksimović

I need many suns,
and at night too,
one to meet me,
one to cast light behind me,
one in a deep precipice,
one to carry in my hand
when from grief I don't see a finger before me.

I need a lot of gentleness,
and every day too,
and a lot of affectionate words;
I need a truce
between the heart and recollections
between the sky
and the pain which kneels before it.

I need many faces
illuminated by welcome,
and every moment too,
I need a friend and a good one,
I need hanging bridges
across hate,
across unbridgeable misunderstanding.

tr. Dasha Čulić Nisula

ПЕСНИКОВ БЛАГОСЛОВ

Desanka Maksimović

На дан моје смрти састаће се они
што почињу тек љубав да слуте;
о поезији мојој младић говориће,
слушаће га девојка главе погнуте.

Тај крај где се живот завршава
учиниће им се топлији од њива,
ведрији од ливада;
почеће девојка први пут да снива.
И младић први пут да се нада.

Учиниће им се да надгробно појање
радосно звони,
и сваки час кроз гробљанско грање
тражиће се погледом они.

Спазићу иза слеђених трепавица,
на које последња светлост пада,
како већ бивају слична
њина лица
и њине руке што ће се тада
машити земље.

И неземаљско моје биће,
што на свету више нема циља,
још једном за собом осврнуће се
да љубав што је на дан смрти никла
узблагосиља.

POET'S BLESSING

by Desanka Maksimović

On the day of my death, only those who
begin to sense love will meet;
the boy will speak of my poetry,
the girl will listen with a bowed head.

That place where life ends
will seem to them warmer than fields,
clearer than meadows;
the girl will for the first time begin to dream.
And the boy will for the first time hope.

It will seem to them that the funeral song
rings happily,
and every moment through the graveyard branches
they will seek each other's gaze.

Behind frozen eyelashes,
on which the last rays fall, I will notice
how their faces already
look alike
and their hands will then
clench a clump of soil.

And my unearthly being,
no longer with an earthly goal,
will turn around one more time
to bless the love that
on the day of death has sprung.

tr. Dasha Čulić Nisula

NDIPO PATAKAMUVIGA PANO
(kumagamba ese akaradzikwa mumasango)

Chirikure Chiriku

Ndipo patakamuviga pano,
    Pano parukangarabwe, muchivavani,
        Pakati pezvimatombo nemiunga,
            Kunge chiya chikara chesango,
                Chisina achazocheuka mangwana.

Ndipo patakamuviga pano,
    Pasure pekunge adauka pamberi pedu,
        Achipika, uku rake gidi richipururudza,
            Akananga kuvhurira vamwe tese nzira,
                Kuti tiwane kubuda parumananzombe.

Ndipo patakamuviga pano,
    Pasure pekunge adamburwa nemhandu,
        Chake chifuva changova mamvemve,
            Iro ivhu ramedza ropa, razvimbirwa,
                Yeduwo isu misodzi ranwa, raguta.

Ndipo patakamuviga pano,
    Amboswera, akavata, katatu,
        Achibinyauka sedora riri muchainga,
            Nyota achipomhodza nemisodzi,
            Nzara achitapudza nemututu.

Ndipo patakamuviga pano,
    Mazuva matatu ekupedzisira tashushana,
        Achiti chindisiyai ndirote zvangu,
            Imi muende mberi neChimurenga;
                Isu tichiti, kwete, tiri tose muhondo.

THIS IS WHERE WE LAID HIM TO REST

by Chirikure Chirikure

This is where we laid him to rest
Right here on this rocky, bare ground
Surrounded by thorny bushes
Here he lies like a wild beast
A brute no one cares about

This is where he lies buried
After he had blazed the trail
Protesting with gunfire
Paving an escape route
For his besieged comrades

This is where we laid him to rest
After the enemy had cut him down
His chest riddled with bullets
The soil red and supple with his blood
Leaving us in tears

This is where he lies buried
After spending three days and nights
Writhing like a worm on fire
Quenching thirst with tears of pain
And hunger with his blood

This is where we laid him to rest
A man we knew nothing about
His name, family or totem
One thing we knew
He was a patriot

Ndipo patakamuviga pano,
Tose tisingazivi kana chimwe chake:
Zita, mhuri, mutupo, kana dzinza,
Zvose kwatiri ichingova mhindo.
Taingoziva: Uyu mwana weivhu!

Ndipo patakamuviga pano,
Pasina ngoma kana mhururu,
Kana muteuro, kana detembo,
Kana chitombo, kana chizhuzhu,
Kana urongwa hwekuzorova guva.

Ndipo patakamuviga pano,
Vake amai vanongova murima,
Vake baba hameno vakarotswa.
Rake dzinza kuti richazochenura?
Chinoziva chete ivhu; mwana rakamedza.

Ndipo paari. Komuredhi Kunozvarwa Vamwe,
Gamba rakaita muchato negidi,
Mhare yakachererwa imba nebhayoneti,
Ndokufukidzwa ivhu nemagaro epfuti,
Ndokuchemwa nezvipuka zvesango.

I-i-i-i-h! Varume!
Ndipo paari pano!
Ndipo ipo pano!

338

This is where he was buried
Without a farewell dance or song
Prayer or eulogy
Without a tombstone

This is where he rests
A fighter who was married to his gun
A hero whose grave we dug with bayonets
Covering it with soil
Scooped with the butts of our guns
A fighter who was mourned
Even by animals of the wild.

tr. Haba Musengezi

Elizabeth Bartlett

A PORTRAIT IN WORDS

It is not easily communicated: where words have become
doors to a world of images, moods, symbols and referents, to
sounds that form a music for the ear tuned to word patterns,
shapes, shadow, and metaphor — words that become prisms to
split the light of the mind into its many possible hues. This is a
variety of human experience known to few, alien to almost all. To
sit for hours at a time to discern the value of a single word, to sense
the weight and worth of the word as a palpable reality, to struggle
against the defects of concentration, the interruptions of everyday
life, to develop an intellectual persistence and aesthetic constancy
that provide a focus for the self and an axis around which one's
daily cares are centered... — These are qualities and habits of mind
decidedly hard to convey. But when they form the innermost
structure of a lifetime, communication in any genuine sense to
another must fail. It is here where living the life of a true poet takes
place, and where words for the non-poet can only point mutely,
and perhaps beckon.

Her life was poetry lived. The poetry that she wrote was the
outer reflection of inner experience, distilled and released from the
particularities of situation and moment. With a discipline and care
born from a deep love and respect for words, their many-leveled
meanings and music, individual poems became for her a means to
compose life's direction and sense.

Elizabeth Bartlett, my mother, was a complex and not
easily understood person. More than anything else, those who met
her for the first time were struck by her intensity and by her fiery
spirit. The continuity of the long thread of her life, her unity of
outlook, her unrelenting energy and dedication all expressed a
deliberately chosen set of values that in her earliest years in New
York City she made the basis for her later life's work.

These values were sensed clearly by anyone who knew her
well. They were dominated by a decisive preference for what is
beautiful in this world, and by a steadfast refusal, and even indig-
nation, that one should ever accept its baseness and ugliness. Her
perspective on life and her commitments in living formed, in other
words, a strongly moral rejection of the dark side of human nature,
on the one hand, and, on the other, a stubborn, unyielding, and
undoubting embrace of the beauty of nature and the beauty of the
human spirit and its creative force. She felt, and was driven by, a

vital respect for the mind's capacity to apprehend, and perhaps at times to invent, the meanings that allow individual men and women to understand and yet never to succumb.

She was a person marked by suffering — in her own life, and in her awareness of the hardships of others. Yet in all that she did, there was a generosity that reflected more than her means, a capacity to love found time and again in sacrifice of self and of professional and personal needs.

Her husband, Paul Alexander Bartlett, was an artist and writer, whose life-long study of the haciendas of Mexico required a gypsy existence of the family. I was their only child. Family life was, to a great extent, held together and cultivated by my mother, who shared and supported her husband's creative work, transmitted intellectual hunger and joy to her son, and made us a family through often nightly readings aloud from great literature of the past, from her husband's writing, and from her own poetry. The burdens of earning a living and making ends meet, in the context of happiness in small things, were most often on her shoulders. For recreation, she loved to play games, especially those involving words. She excelled in Scrabble.

Poetry for my mother was a way of living. Single poems were artifacts of a life lived by a person whose perceptions were highly sensitive to meaningful connections, to the interplay of symbolism, concept, and emotion. It was no accident that following an automobile accident in which she was badly injured, she began to read aloud to her family Hermann Hesse's long novel, *Magister Ludi*. Castalia and the glass bead game were, after all, external realizations of the inherent form of a private life-world devoted to the creation of connections. Evenings over weeks and then months brought the ideals of Castalia into our living room, and also onto tape. It appealed to her lively humor to have recorded what may be the longest reading of a single work.

It is difficult to put the basic ingredients of a richly creative individual's life into a few words. The titles of a few of her seventeen published books, in addition to more than one thousand individually published poems, short stories, and essays, reveal a few lines of a sketch of poetic purpose:

Poems of Yes and No —since at the deepest level the persons we are result from what the individual accepts, and what he rejects;

Threads —a celebration of the intrinsic, manifold continuity of all things;

342

Behold This Dreamer and *The House of Sleep* —because dreamlife and waking life are for this poet not so obviously distinct, nor would she wish them to be;

It Takes Practice Not to Die —for suffering means at least this;

Twelve-Tone Poems —from a composer's love for the music of words, this new form of poetry;

Address in Time, Memory Is No Stranger, and *Around the Clock* —expressing an overpowering personal awareness of that least understood dimension of human experience, time.

Elizabeth Bartlett's poetry has received wide commendation. She is, in a certain sense, "the poet's poet": Her elegant precision in the use of language, her word-crafting skill in meter, structure, and symbolism, and her classical dedication to the universal together place her work on a level that is frequently demanding of the reader, whom she respected, and to whom she would not speak down.

Many of the leaders of this century have praised her work, among them Wallace Stevens, Alfred Kreymbord, John Ciardi, Mark Van Doren, Marianne Moore, Louis Untermeyer, Richard Eberhart, Robert M. Hutchins, William Stafford, Richard Wilbur, Josephine Jacobsen, Robert Hillyer, Allen Tate, Kenneth Rexroth, Conrad Aiken, Gustav Davidson, and many others. A few of their comments have been brought together here:

> *Her poems give one a sense of intelligence and sensibility.*
> — Wallace Stevens

> *I like her poems; they think, and they mean what they say.*
> — Conrad Aiken

> *A fresh, swift, lyrical impulse.... Her poems are mature, they have a bite to them.*
> — Richard Eberhart

> *Any poet might envy the courage and the artistry of what she says, or rather sings.*
> — Alfred Kreymborg

The new form is most interesting, the poems quite beautiful and distinguished.
— Allen Tate, writing about Elizabeth Bartlett's new poetic form, twelve-tone poetry

Clear, swift and strong; and witty, too, in the best sense of that word...
— Mark Van Doren

The poems assuredly justify the writer, and should console the right reader (if anything can).
— Marianne Moore

I am much impressed. The poems seem to me what is called an important contribution, and a beautiful one.
— Robert M. Hutchins

There is a trancelike progression in these poems, in which all unfolds quietly, with a steady holding of a certain pervasive tone... You have accomplished what I keep hoping to do, attaining to continuity between poems and at the same time varying the way of going forward.
— William Stafford

The poems have force, economy, genuineness, and distinctness of tone.
— Richard Wilbur

Elizabeth Bartlett understands that the very large and the very small are siblings. Perceptive and inquiring, her poems ask all our own questions, poems in an original and lucid form.
— Josephine Jacobsen

Elizabeth Bartlett's poems are good examples of the change, or one of the changes in poetry since World War II. They are poems of direct statement, of personal communication, of life, of people, of value relations. Like those of Francis Jammes, Verhaeren, Gertrude Stein, Laura Riding, Reverdy, her poetry is the kind I value, a poetry concerned with the relationships of the self to nature, of self to self, of selves to the world. She has said clearly, 'This is the way I handle life' — and does so superbly.
— Kenneth Rexroth

During the last decade and a half of her life, Elizabeth Bartlett turned to devote her unlimited energy to the advancement of the creative work of other poets. This she did by founding an international project whose purpose is to reinstate the role of literature, and specifically the role of poetry, in the Olympic Games. When the first of the Olympic festivals took place 2,772 years ago in Olympia, Greece, the ancient Greek tradition began of honoring poets, as well as athletes: to award excellence of both Mind and Body.

The ancient Greek Olympiads continued in four year intervals for nearly twelve hundred years until 393 A.D. when Emperor Theodosius of Rome banned the Olympics, which had deteriorated into barbaric carnivals and circuses. That was the 293rd, last Olympiad.

For some fifteen hundred years, the Olympic tradition disappeared from human history. Then, one hundred years ago, in 1896, a Frenchman, Baron de Coubertin, revived the Olympics, but only partially, for the focus was on athletic ability only. The ancient Greek balance, honoring outstanding literary achievements, as well as those of the body, was neglected.

The athletic emphasis in the Olympic Games remained the exclusive one until 1984. In that year, Elizabeth Bartlett published the first international collection of the work of leading contemporary poets, for the purpose of honoring their achievements in the ancient Greek context of the Olympics. Until her death in 1994, Elizabeth Bartlett devoted her time, long hours, and personal finances to the continuation of this project. With the help of a world-wide network of regional associate editors, translators, and an international panel of judges, she edited an international poetry anthology every four years in conjunction with the Olympic Games. A second international anthology was published in 1988, followed by a third in 1992. She was at work on the present anthology, scheduled for publication in 1996, when she died. It was to be the fourth in this series of international poetry anthologies, and to commemorate the 100th year of the modern Olympics.

As the Olympic Games in ancient Greece honored poets for excellence of mind and literary talent, these anthologies paid tribute to leading poets representing the community of world literature. In 1984, they represented nine nations; by 1988, over thirty nations; and in 1992, one hundred thirty-two poets from sixty-five countries. Elizabeth Bartlett believed that "poetry is the voice of the human spirit, wherever it happens to be." Her effort was to restore the ancient Greek balance, to bring poetry back within the Olympic framework of international peace, good will, and celebration of common humanity.

Elizabeth Bartlett was an individual of unusual dedication, a poet with a strong sense of mission, a vision for the future, and the patience and perseverance to realize that vision. With the poetic imagination of Benjamin Franklin, the first to establish endowments to benefit man beyond the compass of a century, she left an inheritance to the future of poetry in the form of a one hundred year trust. When the trust matures, this international endowment for the benefit of poetry in the context of the Greek Olympic ideal will have grown significantly through the compounding effect of time. It will comprise a gift from time itself: time, which throughout her life was perhaps the mystery that called to her most deeply.

Elizabeth Bartlett's large literary collection, consisting of letters, her complete publications, previously unpublished manuscripts, recorded readings, and original poetry-related art, has been donated to the University of California in San Diego, where the Archive for New Poetry is the permanent custodian of the Elizabeth Bartlett Collection.

Steven Bartlett

POETS and TRANSLATORS

Bella Akhmadulina
Born in 1937 in Moscow, Bella Akhmadulina is one of the leading Russian poets. She began publishing verses in 1955, but it was not until 1962 that her first collection, *The String,* appeared in print. Since then she has published numerous collections. A translation of her work came out in 1969 under the title *Fever and Other Poems.* In 1989 she received the State Prize for Literature.

Bisera Alikadić
Bisera Alikadić was born in 1939 in Podhum near Livno, Bosnia. She attended school in Sarajevo. In 1959 she published her first collection of poetry. In addition to over six collections of poetry, she also writes short stories for children and novels. Her work has appeared in numerous anthologies.

Eugenio de Andrade
Clearly the best-known living Portuguese poet, Eugenio de Andrade has published twenty-six volumes of poetry. His work has appeared translated into over twenty languages, with dozens of volumes having appeared in Spain, France and Italy. Alexis Levitin's translations of his work have resulted in seven volumes to date: *Inhabited Heart, White on White, Memory of Another River, Slopes of a Gaze, Solar Matter, The Shadow's Weight,* and *Another Name for Earth.*

Sophia de Mello Breyner Andresen
Sophia de Mello Breyner Andresen's publications include 19 volumes of poetry, two collections of fiction, seven children's books, and three volumes of cultural essays: She is, without a doubt, her country's leading woman-of-letters. Her work has appeared in France, England, Spain, Italy, and Germany. In the United States, Alexis Levitin's translations of her poems have appeared in numerous magazines, including *Prairie Schooner, Chelsea, Translation, Seneca Review, Webster Review, Poetry NOW, Denver Quarterly,* and *Helicon Nine.*

Bjo Ashwill
Born in Oregon, Bjo Ashwill is a fifty-two year old mother, grandmother and a free-lance writer. She worked for ten years at Lane Community College in Eugene, counseling and teaching communication skills. In spite of rheumatoid arthritis, she became a disability activist. In addition to writing poetry and drama, she has self published eight children's books. Many of her works are based on the lives of people with disabilities.

Margaret Atwood
Margaret Atwood is the author of more than twenty-five books of poetry, fiction, and non-fiction. Her newest book, *Morning in the Burned House*, a collection of new poetry, was published by Houghton Mifflin in the spring of 1995. She lives in Toronto, Canada.

Elizabeth Bartlett
Elizabeth Bartlett is the author of seventeen books and more than a thousand individually published poems, short stories, and essays. She is the founder of an international project whose purpose it to reinstate the role of literature, and especially the role of poetry, in the Olympic Games. In 1984 she published the first international collection of the work of leading contemporary poets, for the purpose of honoring their achievements in the ancient Greek context of the Olympics. A second international anthology was published in 1988, followed by a third in 1992. She was at work on the present anthology when she died.

Normand de Bellefeuille
Born in Montreal in 1949, Normand de Bellefeuille has published some twenty books, including *Le Livre du devoir* (Prix de poésie Emile-Nelligan, 1984). *Catégoriques un deux et trois* (Grand prix de poésie de la Fondation des Forges, 1986). *Ce que disait Alice* (Prix Adrienne-Choquette de la nouvelle, 1989), and, more recently, *Obscènes* (Les Editions Herbes Rouges) and *Notte oscura*. In 1979, he co-founded the cultural magazine *Spirale*; between 1984 and 1990, he was eidtor of *La Nouvelle Barre de jour*; and, since 1972, he has been a professor of Quebec Literature. (D.G. Jones's prize-winning translation of *Catégoriques* was published in 1992, as *Categorics, one, two & three*.)

Vizma Belševica
Vizma Belševica was born in Riga, Latvia, in 1931. A member of the Writers' Union of Latvia since 1958, she has authored numerous

collections of poetry and short stories, as well as children's books and translations. Among her fourteen books are *Jura deg* (1966), *Gadu gredzeni* (1969), *Madaras* (1976), *Kamola tineja* (1981), *Dzeltu laiks* (1987); and short stories: *Kikuraga stasti* (1965), *Nelaine majas* (1979) and *Bille* (1992). She is a prolific translator, having translated Shakespeare, Dante, Poe, Twain, Kipling, Hemingway, and Pushkin, among others. Belsevica is an Honorary Member of the Latvian Academy of Science and was awarded the Einar Forseth Foundation Award in 1992, and the Latvian National Three Stars' Order in 1994.

Natalka Bilotserkivets
Natalka Bilotserkivets is a contemporary Ukrainian poet and literary critic who is currently living in Kiev, Ukraine.

Neda Miranda Blažević
Neda Miranda Blažević was born in 1951 in Gračac, Croatia. She studied comparative literature at the University of Zagreb. Artist, poet, novelist and short story writer, Blažević taught creative writing at the University of Minnesota in 1984 and the University of Iowa in 1990. She spent a year in Germany and since 1992 resides in the United States and teaches at St. Catherine's College in St. Paul.

Valentina Borovitskaya
Valentina Borovitskaya is one of the newly heard voices in Russian poetry. She, like other Russian women poets, is beginning to be recognized after the breakup of the former Soviet Union. Her two collections of poetry *Стихи о любви* and *Старинная тетрадь* were published in Moscow, where she lives and works.

George Bowering
George Bowering is a novelist and poet. He was born in British Columbia's Okanagan Valley in 1936. His most recent book of poems, *George Bowering Selected*, edited by Roy Miki, McClelland and Steward, 1993, won the Canadian Author's Association medal and cash for best book of poems for that year.

Fiama Hasse Pais Brandão
Fiama Hasse Pais Brandão has published twelve volumes of poetry and five collections of plays. Her work has been translated into numerous languages, including German, French, Italian, Polish, and English. In the United States, Alexis Levitin's translations of

her poems have appeared in *Partisan Review, Prairie Schooner, The Massachusetts Review, Visions International, Graham Review, Salamander, Seneca Review*, and *Connecticut Poetry Review*. Fiama was a finalist for the European Prize for Literature in 1992.

Mircea Cărtărescu

Born in 1956, Mircea Cărtărescu is perhaps Romania's most important "younger" poet and prose writer of the 1980s "post-modernist" or "blue-jeans" generation. His first book came out in 1980, and he has since published four other volumes, The *Poems of Love* (1983), *Everything* (1985), *The Levant* (1990), and *Love* (1994). Cărtărescu has also written a novel, *The Dream*, and a volume of essays. His works have won major literary awards in Romania and France. Other poems, in co-translation with Adam Sorkin, have appeared in *Another Chicago Magazine, Exquisite Corpse*, and *New Delta Review*.

François Charron

François Charron was born in 1952 in Longueil, Quebec. A prolific writer, he has published in France as well as Quebec and has won numerous prizes, including Le Prix Canada-Belgique. After a long and complex development, his present work is characterized by its extreme spareness and its questioning of many of the truths that pretend to have resolved the human enigma. An experiment in pure affirmation, these poems stand out as some of the most unusual and unsettling poetry there is.

Chirikure Chirikure

Chirikure Chirijure was born in Zimbabwe in 1962. He received a B.A. from the University of Zimbabwe in 1984. In 1990 he attended the famous writer's workshop at the University of Iowa, U.S.A. He has received several awards for his poetry, the most recent being an Honorable Mention in the 1991 Noma Award for Publishing in Africa. He is a prolific writer who cherishes sharing his work with live audiences.

Daniela Crăsnaru

Born in Craiova in 1950, Daniela Crăsnaru is one of Romania's most distinguished and individual poets. A powerful voice, she has over a dozen books to her credit, including both poetry and short fiction, and in 1991 she was honored by being named the winner of the first Romanian Academy prize for career achievement in poetry after the December 1989 revolution. Her most recent book is the 1995 collection of both old and previously unpublished works,

Sixty-Nine Love Poems. A volume of her works came out in the Oxford Poets series (translated by Fleur Adcock); and other poems have appeared in *An Anthology of Romanian Women Poets,* as well as in *Poetry, Prairie Schooner, Michigan Quarterly Review, Visions International, Mangrove, Oxygen,* and *Antigonish Review.*

Anca Cristofovici

Anca Cristofovici was born in Bukarest, Romania in 1956. She emigrated to France in 1985 where she received her Ph.D. from the University of Paris VII in English and American literature. Her first book of translations (with Peter Jay) *The Hour of Sand,* of the Romanian poet Ana Blandiana, was published by Anvil Press in 1990. She is currently working on a study of the American writer John Hawkes.

Katica Ćulavkova

Katica Ćulavkova was born in 1951 in Titov Veles, Macedonia. She completed her studies at the Institute for Literature in Skoplje where she currently works. She has published over five collections of poetry, and her work has appeared in many literary journals, anthologies and has been translated into many languages.

Dasha Čulić Nisula

Dasha Čulić Nisula teaches in the Department of Foreign Languages and Literatures at Western Michigan University. She translates poetry and fiction from various Slavic languages. Her work has appeared in *Cross Currents, International Quarterly, Colorado Review* and *Journal of Croatian* Studies. Her book of poetry in translation, *Selected Poems of Vesna Parun,* was published in 1985.

Vahakn Davtian

Vahakn Davtian is considered to be one of the three leading poets (along with Gevorg Emin and Hamo Sahian) writing in Armenia today. He was born in 1923 in Turkey, after the Allied victory in World War I, when exiled Armenians were allowed to return to their lands. Pogroms began again and his family escaped to Yerevan. Lost land and genocide are constant themes in his poetry. He has edited several literary magazines and was elected president of the new Writers Union in the Republic of Armenia.

Diana Der-Hovanessian

An author of thirteen books of poetry and translation, Diana Der-Hovanessian has won numerous awards for her own and translated works, including prizes from the Poetry Society of America, the

Mary Elinore Smith Prize from American Scholar, NEA and Fulbright scholarships in 1993 and 1994. Her latest book, *Selected Poems of Diane Der-Hovanessian*, Sheep Meadow Press, 1994, was nominated for the Pulitzer Prize. She works as lecturer on American poetry and the poetry of human rights at various universities and serves on the translation board of Columbia University and as president of the New England Poetry Club. Her translations from the work of Maria Banuş, Romanian poet, were published by the *Quarterly Review of Literature* in 1996.

Gabriela Dragnea
Gabriela Dragnea, a graduate of the English Department of the University of Bucharest, is the primary translator of the book-length selection of Marin Sorescu's poems in the Field Translation Series, *Hands Behind My Back* (1991), in collaboration with Stuart Friebert and Adriana Varga. She is also a prose writer who has published short stories in English. Currently she resides in Florence, Italy.

Nancy Eimers
Nancy Eimers was born in Chicago in 1954. She is the author of *Destroying Angel* (Wesleyan University Press, 1991) and has received the Discovery/*The Nation Prize* and a fellowship from the National Endowment for the Arts. She teaches at Western Michigan University and in the MFA program at Vermont College. Her new book of poetry, *No Moon,* will be published by Purdue University Press in summer 1997.

Gevorg Emin
Gevorg Emin is an architect by training who published his first book of poetry the year he graduated from the university and eventually won every literary award given by the former Soviet Union. He is the most widely translated of the living Armenian poets.

Hryhory Falkovych
Hryhory Falkovych is a Jewish-Ukrainian writer living in Kiev, Ukraine. He is best known for his recent book *Spoviduius', vse beru na sebe...* (I confess, I take it all upon me...; Kiev, 1994), in which he deals with the interpenetration of the Jewish and Ukrainian cultures in Ukraine and more recently in Isreal. His meditations largely concern the tragedies of history as well as the poet's intimately lyrical ties to nature in his two homelands.

Madeleine Gagnon

Born in Amqui, Quebec, Madeleine Gagnon has been a teacher of literature and a writer-in-residence in a number of Quebec universities. She is the author of some twenty books of poetry and prose. Her work appears in numerous anthologies and has been translated into several languages. Her books of poetry include *Les fleurs de catalpa* (Prix de poésie du Journal de Montréal, 1986), *Chant pour un Québec lointain* (Prix du Gouverneur général du Canada, 1991) and *La terre est remplie de langage* (1993). A novelist and essayist as well as a poet, she is a member of l'Académie des Lettres du Québec.

Egito Goncalves

Egito Goncalves has published 21 volumes of poetry and has had ten collections of his work appear abroad in France, Spain, Turkey, Poland, Bulgaria, Argentina and Colombia. He himself has translated numerous foreign poets into Portuguese. Alexis Levitin's translations of his work have appeared in *Agni, Artful Dodge, Connecticul Poetry Review, Harvard Review, International Poetry Review, Poetry East, Silverfish Review, The Tennessee Quarterly,* and *Wordsmith.*

Lionello Grifo

Lionello Grifo is a leading Italian poet, winner of the prestigious prize "Premio Lerici-Pea de Poesia 1995." Grifo was born in Rome and started his working life in the worlds of politics and the press. He also worked as a translator. *Whispering: Words in Search of Music* was published in 1980, followed by *Always Whispering: Poetry as Life* in 1989. Part of his trilingual edition of poems won the 'Genti e Paesi' prize in 1990. He has given poetry readings at American and European Universities and in 1989 appeared at the San Francisco National Poetry Week Festival. For the last ten years he has lived in La Manga, in the evocative landscape of Mar Menor in southern Spain.

Dolores Guglielmo

Dolores Guglielmo was born in 1928 in Corona, Long Island, New York. Her work has appeared in print in numerous journals. She won the International Poetry Contest in 1967; in 1983 she received the English Honors Award from Queens College; and in 1992 she was awarded the Writers' Club Award for Excellence in Poetry from Queensborough Community College.

353

Donald Hall

Donald Hall published his twelfth book of poems in 1996, *The Old Life*. He lives in New Hampshire, where he writes essays, short stories, and children's books as well as poems.

Roger Aralamon Hazoume

The nephew of Paul Hazoume, author of *Doguicimi*, Roger Aralamon Hazoume was born in 1944 in Porto-Novo, in Bénin. He studied philosophy and sociology in Paris and teaches currently in Gabon. Hazoume has published two collections of his work, *Fleurs africaines* (1967) and *Le rêve équinoxe d'Orisha Soleil* (1984). His work, which he considers as an engaged work, often reveals both scenic and choreographic influences from the theater.

Ellen C. Hinsey

E.C. Hinsey was born in the United States in 1960. She moved to France in 1987, where she works as a poet, teacher and translator. Her book, *Cities of Memory* won the 1995 Yale Series of Younger Poets Award. Her work has also appeared in *The New England Review, the Southern Poetry Review, the Missouri Review, the Spoon River Poetry Review* and *Fear and the Muse*, an anthology of poetry about the Russian Poet Anna Akhmatova (Zebra Consortium Press, 1996).

Bedros Horasanjian

Bedros Horasanjian is an award winning fiction writer. He was born in 1945 in Bucharest, Romania of Armenian parentage. His poetry, translated from Armenian, is well know in Armenia, but in Bucharest, where he lives and works as an editor and writer, he is best known for his very original prose. He is also the author of an *Encyclopedia of Armenian Writing* in Romanian.

Ioana Ieronim

Ioana Ieronim is the author of seven volumes of poetry as well as a translator and editor. Poems of hers in co-translation with Adam Sorkin have appeared in *Exquisite Corpse, The Literary Review, Antietam Review, Visions International, The Blue Penny Quarterly, Oxford Magazine, The Ohio Poetry Review, Barnabe Mountain Review,* and elsewhere. Until summer 1996, Ms. Ieronim served for four years as Cultural Counselor of the Romanian Embassy in Washington, and she now is head of Public Affairs for the Soros Foundation in Romania.

Nada Iveljić

Nada Iveljić was born in 1931 in Zagreb, Croatia. She completed her literary studies at the University of Zagreb and worked as a professor. Her work has appeared in many literary journals and anthologies. She has published over seven collections of poetry.

Božica Jelušić

Božica Jelušić was born in 1951 in Pitomača, Croatia. She completed her education in Zagreb and works as a teacher and a journalist. In addition to over six collections of poetry, she writes critical essays, stories and translates from English. Her work has appeared in major literary journals and anthologies.

Douglas G. Jones

Douglas G. Jones is an award-winning poet and translator, as well as a literary critic. He taught Comparative Canadian and Quebec Poetry for many years at the Université de Sherbrooke. Retired, he continues to live in North Hatley, Quebec.

Sunny Jung

Born in 1951, Sunny Jung is a Korean poet and translator who is currently teaching Korean language and literature at the University of California, San Diego. She published a book of her Korean poems entitled *The Gate of Zen* in 1981. In 1994 she received both the *Literary Realm* award as well as the *New Poet* award from the Korean Literature Society of America. She studied poetry and translation from the late Elizabeth Bartlett between 1987 and her demise in 1994.

Donald Justice

Donald Justice was born in Miami, Florida, in 1925. He is the author of numerous collections of poetry. He was a Rockefeller Foundation fellow in poetry in 1954; Ford Foundation fellow in 1964; Guggenheim Foundation fellow in 1976; Academy of American Poets fellow in 1988; and a recipient of a Grant from the National Endowment for the Arts in 1967, 1973, 1980 and 1989. He won the Pulitzer Prize in poetry for *Selected Poems* in 1980 and the Bollingen Prize for poems in 1991. He lives and works in Iowa City, Iowa.

Tamara Kazakova

Tamara Kazakova was born in Siberia where she currently lives and publishes her poetry. She is the head of the English Department at the Nizhni Tagil Pedagogical Institute. Recipient of special honors for teaching, Kazakova received an award from the Ministry of Higher Education in 1987. In 1993 she received a Fulbright Scholarship and spent a year in the United States, teaching, lecturing, writing, and translating.

Ilze Kļaviņa Mueller
Born in Latvia, Ilze Kļaviņa Mueller has lived in Germany, Australia and Zaire. She now makes her home in the United States, and teaches German at Macalester College, Saint Paul, Minnesota. A recipient of the Candian Juana Gaita Translation Prize, she has been translating German and Latvian literature since 1970, and is presently at work on an English translation of Anna Brigadere's *Trilogy*.

Stanley Kunitz
Stanley Kunitz was born in Massachusetts in 1905. He completed his undergraduate and graduate studies at Harvard University and taught at numerous universities, among them Brandeis, Columbia, Princeton, and Yale. Kunitz has also lectured abroad in U.S.S.R., Poland, Isreal, Egypt, and Senegal. Recipient of many prestigious awards and fellowships, he is the author of eleven collections of poetry and editor and translator of over a dozen books. He makes his home in New York City.

Patrick Lane
Patrick Lane was born in 1939 in British Columbia. He has traveled widely, working at a variety of jobs from labourer to salesman to teacher. He presently teaches at the University of Victoria. He has published fifteen books of poetry and fiction, including *Poems New and Selected*, which won the Governor General's Award for Poetry in 1978, and the more recent *Winter*. He is currently living in Victoria, B.C. with his companion, the poet Lorna Crozier.

Alexis Levitin
A translator of Brazilian and Portuguese poetry and fiction, Alexis Levitin's work has appeared in well over two hundred literary magazines and journals. His books include Clarice Lispector's *Soulstorm* (New Directions), Carmen Conde's *Woman Without Eden* (translated from the Spanish with José R. de Armas), and seven volumes of poetry by Eugenio de Andrade. He is currently working on an anthology of 20th century Portuguese poetry under a Witter Bynner Poetry Foundation grant.

Desanka Maksimović

Desanka Maksimović was born in 1898 in the village of Rabrovica, near Valjevo, Serbia. She completed her studies in Belgrade and then worked as a teacher. She has published numerous collections of poetry. In addition to writing poetry and prose, Maksimovic translates from Bulgarian, Russian, Slovene, and French. She lives and works in Belgrade.

Ileana Mălăncioiu

Ileana Mălăncioiu was born in Godeni, Romania, in 1940. An important and provocative figure in Romanian literature, over the past thirty years she has published more than thirteen books of poetry. She has won many important prizes including the Romanian Academy Prize and the Romanian Writer's Union Prize. She has also published three books of essays, including a volume of political essays published after 1989, which received the Writers' Union Prize in Journalism. For many years she worked as the editor of *Viata Romaneasca*, one of Romania's most important literary journals.

Daphne Marlatt

Daphne Marlatt was born in Melbourne, Australia, and spent her childhood in Malaysia, before arriving in Vancouver, British Columbia. She is a novelist as well as a poet, and an itinerant lecturer in English, Women's Studies, and Liberal Studies. A major long poem centered on a West Coast fishing village is *Steveston* (1974). Recent titles include *Ghost Works* and *Salvage*, as well as the novel *Ana Historic*.

Attila Mohylny

Attila Mohylny was born in Kiev, Ukraine, in 1963. He completed his philology degree at Kiev State University and continued his studies in Dushanbe, Tadzhikistan. Upon returning to Kiev in 1985, he worked as a journalist and teacher at Kiev and Warsaw universities. He is the author of two books of poetry: *Rattling Above the Rooftops* (1987) and *Countours of the City* (1991). He is currently preparing his third book of poetry for publication and writing short stories and a novel.

Quentin Ben Mongaryas

Born Jean-Claude Quentin in 1948 in Gabon, Quentin Ben Mongaryas has received numerous poetry awards. He did his secondary schooling in a technical school, and worked with Gabonese Telecommunications between 1967 and 1975. In 1976,

357

Mongaryas was named First Advisor to the Ambassador to Gabon in West Germany. His writing has been described at times as volcanic and disconcerting.

Haba Musengezi
Haba Musengezi is a playwright, novelist, poet and translator from Zimbabwe who currently resides in the United States.

Michael M. Naydan
Michael M. Naydan teaches in the Department of Slavic and East European Languages at the Pennsylvania State University. He has published numerous translations of poetry from Russia for which he received several awards. He also translates Ukrainian poets. His work has appeared in various journals and anthologies, most recently in *Contemporary Women Poets of the World* and *Shifting Borders: Eastern European Poetries of the Eighties.*

Viktor Neborak
Born in 1961, Viktor Neborak is one of the leading members of the Bu-Ba-Bu performance-oriented literary group from Lviv, Ukraine and has performed as well as a punk and rock musician. He is largely responsible for the Ukrainian literary renaissance in Western Ukraine from the mid-1980s to the present as a poet-performer, as well as a tireless promoter of indigenous Ukrainian culture. He is best known for his collections of poetry *Litaiucha holova* (Flying Head; Kiev, 1990), which marks the pinnacle of his carnivalizing verse, and the intentionally more subdued *Alter Ego* (Kiev, 1993).

Charles Nokan
Charles Nokan is a poet, novelist, and playwright from the Ivory Coast. Born Konon Kouamé in 1936 in Yamoussoukro, he has been a professor of sociology and philosophy at the University of Abidjan since 1974. His works center on the depiction and study of Africa from a variety of perspectives, all the while preferring that of the heroic viewpoint.

Se-young Oh
Born in 1942, Se-young Oh is a well-known Korean poet, a leading literary critic and a professor at Seoul National University. His debut through *Hyonde Munhak* in 1968 was honored with *Sowol Si Munhak Sang* and *Hankuk SihyopSang*. His books include *The Other Side of Love, A Foolish Hegel,* and *A Shadow of Sky in the*

Tears. He expresses Eastern thinking with the techniques of modernism.

William Olsen

William Olsen has published two books of poetry, *The Hand of God and a Few Bright Flowers* (a National Poetry Series Selection), and *Vision of a Storm Cloud* (Triquarterly Press). His awards include a National Endowment for the Arts Fellowship, a YHMA/Nation Discovery Award, a Breadloaf Fellowship, a *Pushcart* Prize, the *Poetry Northwest* Helen Bullis Prize, and a *Crazyhorse* Poetry Award. He teaches at Western Michigan University and Vermont College.

P.K. Page

Author and painter, P.K. Page has published over a dozen books of poetry, fiction, and non-fiction, winning various awards, including the Governor General's Award for Poetry, while her painting has been exhibited internationally and is represented in the permanent collections of The National Gallery, the Art Gallery of Ontario, and other museums. Her latest book of poems is *Hologram* (1994). Having traveled widely for much of her life, she now makes her home in Victoria, B.C.

Wanda Phipps

Wanda Phipps is a poet and a recipient of a New York Foundation for the Arts Poetry Fellowship. She and Virlana Tkacz were awarded the Agni Translation Prize for Poetry and the National Theatre Translation Fund Award for their work on the classic verse drama *The Forest Song.* Their work has appeared in *Agni Review, Visions International, Beacons, Our Life* and *Index on Censorship.*

Ivana Rangel-Carlsen

Ivana Rangel-Carlsen was born in Brazil and came to the United States on a scholarship to study at the University of California in Berkeley and Santa Barbara. During the past ten years she has published translations of prose and poetry of Miguel Torga as well as other Portuguese writers. She presently lives in Puerto Vallarta, Mexico.

Jean-Claude Renard

Jean-Claude Renard, born in 1922, has won many prizes, including the Grand Prix de Poésie de l'Académie Française (1988). His poetic practice displays a wide range of techniques; he often favors free verse, whether based on short lines or on a longer unit that approaches prose. Renard, who lives in Paris and spends part of each summer in Saint-Pierre-de-Chartreuse, has lectured throughout the world; he is a member of the Académie Mallarmé. *Jean-Claude Renard: Selected Poems*, edited by Graham Dustan Martin, was published in 1978.

Tyyne Saastamoinen

Tyyne Saastamoinen was born in Finland in 1921 in Vyborg, the Carelian capital, which was annexed by the Soviet Union in 1945. She has lived in France since 1960. Her work is haunted by memory, ephemeral time and the difficulties of exile. From *The Icon and the Apple* (1954) and *Glaciation* (1962) to *The European* (1972, 1986), she has spoken of contemplation, hope, and nostalgia. She has published seventeen volumes, the most recent being *You Know, Time* (1994).

Gloria de Sant'Anna

Gloria de Sant'Anna was born in Portugal in 1925. As a young woman she went to Mozambique where she was a housewife and school teacher. Following the independence of that African nation, she was forced to return to Portugal in 1979 where she still lives, largely unresigned to what she calls her "exile." She is one of the most revered voices in the literary panorama of Mozambique and has published seven books of poetry. The book *Amaranth* was published in 1988 and includes poetry written between 1951 and 1983.

Catharine Savage Brosman

Catharine Savage Brosman, who is the Kathryn B. Gore–Professor of French at Tulane University, has written widely on the literary history of France in the twentieth century, especially ideological fiction. Her most recent scholarly book is *French Culture 1900-1975* (Detroit: Gale, 1995). In addition, she has published a collection of autobiographical essays, *The Shimmering Maya and Other Essays* (Louisiana State University Press, 1994), and four collections of poetry, of which the most recent is *Passages* (LSU Press, 1996).

Eric Sellin

Eric Sellin is a professor of French at Tulane University in New Orleans. His collections of poetry include *Night Voyage* (1964), *Trees at First Light* (1973), *Nightfall over Lubumbashi* (1982), and *Dean of Noon* (1992), as well as two books of poems composed in

French, *Borne kilométrique* (1973) and *Crépuscule prolongé à El-Biar* (1982).

Suzanne Shipley

Suzanne Shipley teaches in the Department of Germanic Languages and Literatures at the University of Cincinnati. She has published translation in *New Orleans Review, Sulphur*, and *Dimension*.

Soo-Kwan Song

Born in 1940, Soo-Kwan Song is a leading Korean poet who was honored with the Munhak Sansang Award in 1975, and later with the prestigious Sowol Si Munhak Sang award. His books include *Leaning Against the Mountain Gate, A Dreaming Island,* and *Our Earth.* He uses the local color of Korean scenes for his poetic subjects. His poems seek to express the harmony between humans and nature.

Marin Sorescu

Marin Sorescu was born in 1936. He graduated with a university degree in philology in 1960, having already published some of the parodies and pastiches that make up his first book, *Alone Among Poets* (1964). Among his more than twenty volumes are *Fountains in the Sea* (1982), *Water of Life, Water of Death* (1987), *Poems Selected by Censorship* (1991), and *Crossing* (1994). Sorescu is also a prolific writer of drama. Five of his plays have appeared in English translations, and his treatrical works have been produced throughout Europe. In late 1993, Sorescu was appointed Romanian Minister of Culture, a position he held until spring 1995.

Adam J. Sorkin

Adam J. Sorkin has been called by *The Literary Review* "one of this country's leading translators of Romanian poetry." His collaborative translations of contemporary Romanian poets have appeared in over ninety literary and poetry magazines. In 1994, he published two books of Romanian poetry, *An Anthology of Romanian Women Poets* and *Transylvanian Voices: An Anthology of Contemporary Poets from Cluj-Napoca.* He put into print two other books of Romanian translations, *Fires on Waters* and *Love and Winter.* Sorkin's fifth book, *The Sky Behind the Forest*, was published in 1996. He teaches as a Professor of English at the Delaware Country Campus of Penn State.

Victoria Stakh

Victoria Stakh was born in Kiev in 1969 and studied linguistics. She is the author of the collection *Meeting Near the Transformer* (1991) and the editor of *The White Book of Love,* an anthology of 20th century Ukrainian erotic poetry (1990). Her poems have been performed in several theatre workshops at Harvard Summer School. Currently, she lives in Kiev and works as the poetry editor for the journal *Ukraina.*

Mirela Surdulescu

Mirela Surdulescu, a 1970 graduate in English of the University of Bucharest, teaches English in Bucharest's English high school. She has published in a variety of forms: her own poetry; translations into English; translations into Romanian (including Wordsworth, Kipling, and Auden); and articles on teaching English, on Ireland, and on Saul Bellow.

Radu Surdulescu

Radu Surdulescu teaches in the English Department of the University of Bucharest; in 1994-95 he was at Duke University on a Fulbright grant. He is an important critic and translator of criticism into Romanian. Works by three Romanian poets other than Cartarescu, in his versions with Adam Sorkin, have appeared in *Visions International* and *Confrontation.* Professor Surdulescu is currently finishing his doctorate, having been forbidden by the Communist authorities to pursue an advanced degree because he had been a political prisoner as a student.

Marilena Tamburello

Marilena Tamburello is a linguist and translator with two doctoral degrees: one in English and American Literature from Italy, and one in Linguistics and Comparative Literature from Seattle, Washington. She has taught English as a Second Language at Stanford University, City College, and St. Mary's College in San Francisco. She currently lives in Berkeley, California.

Ludmyla Taran

Born in 1954, Ludmyla Taran studied literature at Kiev University and has been a member of the Writers' Union since 1984. Currently, she works at the Rylsky Literary Museum in Kiev. Her books of poetry include *Deep Leaves* (1982), *Watermarks* (1985), *Rafters* (1990), and *Defending the Soul* (1994). She has also published a collection of literary essays, *Energy in Search* (1988). Her poem "India Ink" was included in Yara Art Group's theatre piece *Waterfall/Reflections* performed at La Mama in New York and at Kiev's Experimental Theatre Festival.

Jean-Baptiste Tati-Loutard

Born in Ngoyo (Congo) in 1938, Jean-Baptiste Tati-Loutard is a professor at Marien Ngouabi University in Brazzaville. For many years he also served as his country's Minister of Culture and Scientific Research. He is the author of a prize-winning novel, *Le Récit de la mort* (1987), short stories, and numerous books of poems, including *Le Dialogue des plateaux* (1982), *La Tradition du songe* (1985), *Le Serpent australe* (1992), and *L'Ordre des phénomènes, suivi de Les Feux de la planète* (1996) in which the poems here translated first appeared.

Virlana Tkacz

Virlana Tkacz and Wanda Phipps were awarded the Agni Translation Prize for Poetry and the National Theatre Translation Fund Award for their work on the classic verse drama *The Forest Song.* Their work has appeared in *Agni Review, Visions International, Beacons, Our Life* and *Index on Censorship.* Virlana Tkacz also heads the Yara Arts Group which is a resident company of La Mama Experimental Theatre in New York.

Mona Van Duyn (Mrs. Jarvis Thurston)

Mona Van Duyn was born in Waterloo, Iowa, in 1921, and since 1950 has lived in St. Louis. She has taught widely in the United States and abroad, most recently at Washington University. She has received many prizes and awards for her poetry, including the National Book Award, the Bollingen Prize and the Pulitzer Prize. Washington University, Cornell College, the University of Northern Iowa, George Washington University, Georgetown University, and the University of the South have awarded her the degree of Honorary Doctor of Letters. In June of 1992 she was appointed by the Librarian of Congress as Poet Laureate Consultant in Poetry.

Heini Vartia-Delafont

Heini Vartia-Delafont was born in Finland in 1947 in Helsinki. She has lived in France for twenty-eight years, and has spent the last ten years renovating a 13th century castle in the Cevennes region of southern France. She is a translator, painter and acupunctor and regularly leads Chinese painting workshops in France and Finland.

Saša Vegri
Saša Vegri is a pseudonym for Albina Doberšek, married Vodopivec. She was born in 1937 in Belgrade, and has published numerous collections of poetry. Her work has appeared in various anthologies and has been translated into many languages. She lives and works in Ljubljana, Slovenia.

Lidia Vianu
Lidia Vianu, an accomplished translator as well as a novelist and critic, works in the English Department of the University of Bucharest. In 1991-92 she lectured at SUNY Binghamton on a Fulbright grant. Professor Vianu's translations (most with Adam Sorkin) have come out in *The American Poetry Review, The Literary Review, New Virginia Review, The Berkeley Poetry Review, Marquee, Potomac Review, Poetry Motel, Nimrod, Romanian Civilization, Visions International, 100 Words, Times Literary Supplement,* and *Exquisite Corpse.*

Edd Wheeler
Edd Wheeler is a federal administrative law judge who has published poetry extensively. In 1994 he edited a book of poetry entitled *Ornaments of Fire,* and in 1996 his book on the Olympic games, *From Games of God to Bubba's Field*, was published by Heath Row Press.

Richard Wilbur
In 1987-8, Richard Wilbur served as the nation's second Poet Laureate, and in the latter year received the Pulitzer prize for his *New and Collected Poems.* Among his recent translations of Molière are the *School for Husbands* and *Amphitryon.*

Stephanie Yang
Stephanie Yang is a graduate student in French literature and film at Tulane University. She is an avid writer of both short fiction and poetry, having published several poems in national anthologies and university literary journals. In addition to her writing in English, she is a writer of poetry and prose in French and a translator of French and Francophone poetry into English.

Oksana Zabuzhko
Born in 1960 in Lutsk, Ukraine, Oksana Zabuzhko is considered one of the best writers of her generation. Her collections of poetry include *May Frost* (1985), *Conductor of the Last Candle* (1990),

and *Hitchhiking* (1994). She has translated the poetry of Sylvia Plath into Ukrainian and has been a writer-in-residence at Harvard, Penn State University and the University of Pittsburgh. Currently, she lives in Kiev and is a member of the Writers' Union.

Anka Žagar

Anka Žagar was born in Zamost, Croatia in 1954. She graduated from the University of Zagreb in Yugoslav Languages and Comparative Literature. Her first collection of poetry was published in 1983, and her sixth collection was published in 1992. She lives and works in Zagreb.

Ifigenija Zagoričnik

Ifigenija Zagoričnik was born in 1953 in Ljubljana, Slovenia. She completed her studies in Slavistics and Comparative Literature at the University of Ljubljana. In London she completed studies in ceramics at the Harrow College of Art and Design. She has published over seven collections of poetry and has been represented in many anthologies. She lives and works in London.

Annemarie Zornack

Annemaire Zornack was born in 1932 in Aschersleben in the Harz, West Germany. Zornack holds a leading place among German women writers of the eighties. Winner of the 1979 Friedrich-Hebbel prize for poetry, her publications include *kusshand, Die langbeinige Zikade, treibanker werfen*, as well as numerous prose works.

* * * * * * * * * *

About the Artist: **Josip Banovac**

Josip Banovac was born in Split, Croatia in 1958. He completed his studies in Split, where he continues to live, work and exhibit in individual and group shows. His collection of sculptures of athletes in polyester are characteristic of hellenistic sculptures in clear form but without the details of musculature. They represent in geometric perfection the dynamism of motion. These sculptures were first exhibited in Split in 1990.

ACKNOWLEDGMENTS

NANCY EIMERS: "A History of Navigation" and "A Night Without Stars" appeared *No Moon*, Purdue University Press, 1997. Reprinted with permission of the poet and Purdue University Press.

DONALD HALL: "A Beard for a Blue Pantry" first appeared in *Poetry*, Februa 1995. Reprinted with the permission of the Editor of *Poetry*.

"The Hunters" first appeared in *The New Republic*. Reprinted w the permission of Laura Obolensky, Rights and Permissions, *New Republic*.

"The Porcelain Couple" first appeared in the January 22, 1996 is of *The New Yorker*. Reprinted with the permission of the poet *The New Yorker*.

"Weeds and Peonies" first appeared in *The New York Ti Magazine*, December 31, 1995. Reprinted with the permissio the poet.

DONALD JUSTICE: "Pantoum of the Great Depression" appeared in *New and Sele Poems*, Knopf, 1995. Reprinted with the permission of the and Random House, Inc.

STANLEY KUNITZ: "Halley's Comet," and "My Mother's Pears" first appeared in *New Yorker*, October 9, 1995 and May 17, 1993, respecti Reprinted with the permission of the poet and *The New Yorker*.

MONA VAN DUYN: "Mr. and Mrs. Jack Sprat in the Kitchen" appeared in *Fir Knopf, 1993. Reprinted with the permission of the poet Random House, Inc.

RICHARD WILBUR: "A Barred Owl" was originally published in *Sewanee Theole Review* (35:2, Easter 1992), published by the School of The of the University of the South. Reprinted with the permission poet and the managing editor of the *Sewanee Theological Revi*